EDGELANDS

Paul Farley is the author of four collections of
poetry and has received the Forward Prize for
Best First Collection, the Whitbread Poetry Award
and the E.M. Forster Award from the American
Academy of Arts and Letters.

Michael Symmons Roberts has published five
collections of poetry – including *Corpus*, which
won the Whitbread Poetry Award – and two
novels. He is a frequent collaborator with the
composer James MacMillan, and their opera 'The
Sacrifice' won the RPS Award.

Edgelands won a Royal Society of Literature
Jerwood Award for non-fiction in 2009

PAUL FARLEY
AND
MICHAEL SYMMONS ROBERTS

Edgelands

Journeys into England's True Wilderness

VINTAGE BOOKS
London

Published by Vintage 2012

2 4 6 8 10 9 7 5 3

First published in Great Britain in 2011 by
Jonathan Cape

Vintage
Random House, 20 Vauxhall Bridge Road,
London SW1V 2SA

www.vintage-books.co.uk

Addresses for companies within The Random House Group Limited
can be found at:
www.randomhouse.co.uk/offices.htm

The Random House Group Limited Reg. No. 954009

A CIP catalogue record for this book
is available from the British Library

ISBN 9780099539773

The Random House Group Limited supports The Forest Stewardship
Council (FSC®), the leading international forest certification organisation.
Our books carrying the FSC label are printed on FSC® certified paper.
FSC is the only forest certification scheme endorsed by the leading
environmental organisations, including Greenpeace. Our
paper procurement policy can be found at
www.randomhouse.co.uk/environment

MIX
Paper from
responsible sources
FSC® C016897

Printed and bound in Great Britain by Clays Ltd, St Ives PLC

Contents

Introduction

'Une ville, une campagne, de loin, c'est une ville et une campagne, mais à mesure qu'on s'approche, ce sont des maisons, des arbres, des tuiles, des feuilles, des herbes, des fourmis, des jambes de fourmis, à l'infini. Tout cela s'enveloppe sous le nom de campagne.'

Pascal, *Pensées*

['A city, a countryside from a distance is a city and a countryside; but as you approach, they are houses, trees, shingles, leaves, grass, ants, legs of ants, and so on to infinity: all this is enveloped in the name "countryside".']

In the English imagination, the great escape might go something like this: you get into your car, merge into traffic, and join a busy motorway via one of the feeder roads from the city; after an hour or two, you leave at the correct junction and join an A-road, which you follow for a while before turning off on to smaller, quieter roads that elide into narrow lanes; eventually, the lane dips and climbs through wooded hollows, affording sudden views as it follows the line of a ridge, then descends to a track where an ivy-clad cottage waits, a light burning in its window; the key is under the mat, you notice the cottage has a name rather than a number ('Albion'); you let yourself in to its

1

cool, wainscoted hallway, where a clock ticks and time runs backwards.

For a long while, an entire childhood in fact, we wondered where the countryside actually was, or even if it really existed. Growing up on the edge of two cities – Liverpool and Manchester – in the early Seventies, it was easy enough to walk for a short while and soon find yourself lost in back lanes or waste ground, to follow the wooded perimeters of a golf course, an old path leading through scratchy shrubland, or the course of a drainage ditch. It was easy enough to find yourself on the edges of arable land, to follow the track bed of a dismantled railway or descend into an abandoned quarry. But none of this ever really felt like the countryside: the sunlit uplands of jigsaw puzzles and Ladybird books, the rolling hills of biscuit-tin lids, the meadowlands and glades in the framed, reproduced pastorals our parents hung on our living-room walls or that we saw on television or read about.

We were sceptical, to a point at which we wondered whether this Elsewhere was in fact a total fiction, lit and staged in the same way the moon landings a few years earlier had been confected. Though not even the CIA could invent a character like Jack Hargreaves, from the then long-running TV series *Out of Town*. We loved Jack. Whether he was tying his own flies for trout, lamping for rabbits on moonless nights or dipping a horseshoe into the hissing water of a dark smithy, Jack was all we had to go on, proof positive that the countryside was a real place that still existed. But how did you get there?

*

In *Drosscape*, Alan Berger's study of the vast, uncharted geography of waste landscapes and urban sprawl in the United States, a problem of definition arises. Berger took to the air in a Cessna to explore the horizontal city in an attempt to understand a complex and fast-moving new terrain. He collected many names for the urbanisation of landscape, and almost as if to keep up with the space and scale of American waste, language had obligingly proliferated:

boomburb
citistate
datascape
dead city
deconcentration
dispersed city
distributive protocols
dual city
dumpspace
edge city
edgeless city
enclaves
ephemeral city
exploding metropolis
Fordist city
galactic metropolis
global city
global-dual city
informal city
informational city
junkspace
landscape urbanism
limitless city
linked city

megalopolis

micropolis

midopolis

minicentre

multicentred metropolitan region

multinucleated metropolitan region

negative space

nerdistan

network urbanism

off worlds

peripheral city

polycentric city

polynucleation

post-city

post-Fordist city

smart growth

splintering urbanism

sprawl

stimdross

suburban sprawl

technoburb

technopolis

transurbanism

urbalism

urban sprawl

vanishing city

world city

We might have come up with the word 'edgelands' ourselves.
Anyone who has spent a childhood mooching around the fringes of

English towns and cities, where urban and rural negotiate and renegotiate their borders, might have come up with the word. If you know those places where overspill housing estates break into scrubland, wasteland; if you know these underdeveloped, unwatched territories, you know that they have 'edge'. We *might* have come up with it ourselves, but geographer Marion Shoard got there first. Her writing on England's edgelands, her call to arms, for poets and novelists to celebrate them, and above all her *naming* of this ground was the starting point for us. The writer Georges Perec once observed that the Eskimo's famously plenteous vocabulary for types of snow and ice is not repeated in words to describe the spaces between their igloos, while in English we have an abundance of words to account for the variety of landscapes on our doorstep, in our built environment. Hopefully, we can help introduce one more into circulation.

So much might depend on being able to *see* the edgelands. Giving them a name might help, because up until now they have been without any signifier, an incomprehensible swathe we pass through without regarding; untranslated landscape. And edgelands, by and large, are not meant to be seen, except perhaps as a blur from a car window, or as a backdrop to our most routine and mundane activities. Edgelands are part of the gravitational field of all our larger urban areas, a texture we build up speed to escape as we hurry towards the countryside, the distant wilderness. The trouble is, if we can't see the edgelands, we can't imagine them, or allow them any kind of imaginative life. And so they don't really exist. The smaller identities of things in the edgelands have remained largely invisible to most of us.

This book's other presiding spirit is Richard Mabey and *The Unofficial Countryside*. First published in 1973, Mabey's wonderful study must have opened many eyes to the vitality and worth of urban edges in England, though his focus was on the resilience of nature in these waste places, rather than a celebration of the places themselves. Mabey didn't necessarily cherish these new habitats in their own right, or seek 'to excuse the dereliction, the shoddiness and the sheer wastefulness of much of our urban landscape'.

Everyone knows – after a sentence or two of explanation – their local version of the territories defined by this word 'edgelands'. But few people know them well, let alone appreciate them. Our book is an attempt to celebrate these places, to break out of the duality of rural and urban landscape writing, to explore these unobserved parts of our shared landscape as places of possibility, mystery, beauty.

*

As poets in the English lyric tradition, we are drawn to the idea of praise, of celebration. And we are equally aware of its difficulty. The edgelands are a complex landscape, a debatable zone, constantly reinventing themselves as economic and social tides come in and out. Of course, the idea of edgelands does not just refer to parts of the physical environment. It's a rich term for poetry, too, and can maybe help to break down other dualities. Poets have always been attracted by the overlooked, the telling details, the captured moment. And the moment is important here, too. If parts of remote rural Britain feel timeless (though this feeling is, of course, illusory) then the edgelands feel anything but. Revisit an edgelands site you haven't seen for six months, and likely as not there will be a Victorian factory knocked down, a business park newly built, a section of waste ground cleared and landscaped, a pre-war warehouse abandoned and open to the elements. Such are the constantly shifting sands of edgelands that any writing about these landscapes is a snapshot. There is no definitive description of the edgelands of Swindon, or Wolverhampton, only an attempt to celebrate and evoke them at one particular time.

Time and again, we found a place that is as difficult to pin down and define as poetry, but like poetry, you'd know it when you saw it. It often contained decay and stasis, but could also be dynamic and deeply mysterious. Edgelands are always on the move. In our own lifetimes, we've noticed how they have changed, largely as a result of the big push for the motorways and the rise of out-of-town shopping, as retailers shifted their operations to the huge floor space and parking opportunities available on the margins of our cities. Such developments tend to perpetuate further development, as infrastructure forms its busy threads of connective tissue, and the course of existing roads is altered, like light bending towards a black hole. The rudely functional big sheds of retail, their battle-ship greys festooned with the primary colours of brand names and logos, were largely unknown to us thirty-odd years ago, as were the reinvented spaces of the outlet village.

We remembered a kind of Arcadia. The Lancashire edgelands we explored and played in as children were formed in some of the wider spaces of dereliction and waste left behind in the aftermath of industrialisation. Visiting Lancashire a generation earlier in the Thirties, J. B. Priestley had written: 'Between Manchester and Bolton the ugliness is so complete that it is almost exhilarating. It challenges you to live there.' As we grew up, the chimneys came down, the slag and spoil heaps were shifted or landscaped, and the lie of the land had begun to appear less raw than it had done to another Thirties visitor, George Orwell. In this cooling wake, a less apocalyptically ugly landscape was emerging, haphazardly, beyond the edges of our towns and cities, which themselves were growing outwards in the post-war rush to throw up cheap, high-density housing. But it was a new landscape that made no sense, one with no obvious artistic or literary analogue, no rhyme or reason.

At their most unruly and chaotic, edgelands make a great deal of our official wilderness seem like the enshrined, ecologically arrested, controlled garden space it really is. Children and teenagers, as well as lawbreakers, have seemed to feel especially at home in them, the former because they have yet to establish a sense of taste and boundaries, and have instinctively treated their jungle spaces as a vast playground; the latter because nobody is looking.

*

We made many journeys into this landscape, though this isn't a book of walks, rambles, dérives or flâneurisms. Although elements of all these things undoubtedly helped us reacquaint ourselves with this no-man's-land, both of us already knew this landscape well, having grown up living close to it. The things to be found and experienced in this zone – indeed, the unkempt and overlooked textures of this zone in its entirety – have already found their various ways into many of the poems, dramas and stories we've both written since. We knew this place intimately, long before we decided to write at length upon it.

There have been many artists and writers who have been drawn to this new landscape, and their work has helped us look again and in different ways. Nevertheless, we felt that the edgelands were being largely ignored or misrepresented in the explosion of landscape writing in the last decade. Sometimes they are written off as part of the urban (or suburban) human landscape that has to be escaped, or transcended, in order to discover true solitude in the wilds of northern Scotland, or on the fringes of our island archipelago. At other times – as in the work of some so-called *psychogeographers* – they are merely a backdrop for bleak observations on the mess we humans have made of our lives, landscapes, politics and each other. In our view, both these 'schools' run the same risk – using the edgelands as a short cut to misanthropy.

We decided to write the book together in the anonymous tradition. Subsuming both of our voices seemed like a good way of getting into this territory. This was a difficult landscape to immerse ourselves in physically – there would be no tree climbing, and swimming in standing water was out of the question – though in the backs of our minds there was a sense of letting the terrain speak for itself, rather than framing ourselves within it as intrepid explorers. We also felt joint authorship might lead us from the well-trodden path of stick-waving or professional outsiderdom. Letting a complacent and hypnotised hoi polloi know how we could see through the mirage didn't interest us, not least because, the more we travelled through and thought about this landscape, the more we found we admired it.

Geographically, this is a wide picture, reflecting journeys we have made to the north, south, east and west of England. But we were both born and raised in England's north-west, the former industrial heartland stretching from Liverpool to Manchester. And we both – after periods living and working in London and elsewhere in the British Isles – have come home to the north-west in recent years. So, although our travels and observations are wide-ranging, our deepest emotional connection is with the edgelands around those great rival cities of Manchester and Liverpool, and that is reflected in the book.

The book gradually took shape around *things* to be found in this debatable region, although such a discrete organisation should fool no one: on the ground, particularly rich tracts of edgelands can be found containing many, if not all, of our chapter subjects, side by side and often overlapping with each other. But in concentrating our attention upon individual facets and characteristics, pausing to describe, explore and imagine, and taking something akin to a meditative approach, we hope the chapters rhyme enough to suggest correspondences and commonalities, and that their boundaries, at least a little like the real thing, remain porous.

*

Somewhere in the hollows and spaces between our carefully managed wilderness areas and the creeping, flattening effects of global capitalism, there are still places where an overlooked England truly exists, places where ruderals familiar here since the last ice sheets retreated have found a way to live with each successive wave of new arrivals, places where the city's dirty secrets are laid bare, and successive human utilities scar the earth or stand cheek by jowl with one another; complicated, unexamined places that thrive on disregard, if we could only put aside our nostalgia for places we've never really known and see them afresh.

Cars

The poet and sage Roy Fisher has described a gradual shift in his view of his home city, Birmingham: 'The landscape has come, with the passage of time and changes in my understanding, to moralise itself under my eye, without any nudging from me. I read it as a record of conduct as well as something subjectively transfigured.'

He's right, of course, but cities aren't the only records of our conduct. The remotest Scottish Highlands have our political, economic and social history written all over them, and the edgelands are no different.

Take a walk through any of our edgelands and the landscape paints itself as a *paysage moralisé*. On second thoughts, don't take a walk, take a drive. The edgelands are to drive for, to, through. This is where cars come into their own, and not just executive coupés on their way to business meetings.

*

Cars are a defining characteristic of the edgelands. Here you can have them re-sprayed, re-tyred, re-tuned. But there is another auto-ritual carried out here, a ritual that begins with an empty space on a city street. After rage, panic and complex reordering of the rest of the day, the errant driver has to cadge a lift or hail a taxi to the edgelands, on the trail of a towed-away car. That decision to park for five minutes on a double yellow line leads to an expensive trip out of the city centre, to a compound ringed by steel fences topped with barbed wire. The driver is dropped off, pays the taxi, and takes the walk of shame and fury. The driver is dressed for a day in the city, not for the clamper's yard. The driver picks a path through rainbow pools of drizzle and petrol. There is usually an argument, but this is pointless. The clamper, behind his metal grille in the bare office, has heard it all a thousand times before, and doesn't even bother to turn the radio down. He simply repeats, calmly as a litany, the nature and location of the sin, and the wages due because of it. Eventually, the driver pays a huge fee in return for a set of directions – three rows down, towards the back of the yard – and is let out of the gate with a thumbs up. Hours late for meetings, hundreds of pounds the poorer, paying the price in blood pressure, the driver speeds away from the edgelands, back to the anonymous city.

*

On summer nights, the edgelands become the domain of boy racers and their newly pimped rides. Some are there to put their souped-up engines through their paces, roaring down the long straight strips, burning rubber in the empty car parks. Others are there to park with doors open, lid lifted on a polished engine, oversized sound system cranked up full. These cars are electric purple, crimson, lurid green. They don't just have lights, they have lights on their lights – massive spots that drain the battery if left on too long, disco lights on the back parcel shelf. Best of all, they have mysterious blue lights underneath the chassis, so at night they seem to float in an electric-blue pool of their own making. These cars are born again. Third- or fourth-hand, they changed owners for hundreds, not thousands. Then one day, a customiser spotted them, the old Capris and Golfs, the former rep cars and hot hatches. Someone saw their potential, and was willing to sink hours and pounds into giving them another heyday. Mutton dressed as lamb, they stand in resolute defiance of government scrappage schemes, ecological maxims, the laws of suburban driving. These are edgelands chimeras, beautiful, garish freaks.

*

But not all cars are born again. The edgelands are also a graveyard for cars. This is not for the squeamish. Passers-by on trains, avert your eyes. This is the end of the road, and your beloved weekend runabout is destined to breathe its last here. It's a classic scene from thrillers and Seventies cop shows: the chase that ends in a capture in a car-crusher's yard, the huge hydraulic claw picking up the car with driver still inside, the hapless victim unable to jump free as the car is dropped in to the crusher, the screams as the crusher walls close on the car, the magnet on a chain lifting the resultant cube and dropping it on a heap of other cubes. But on a tour of edgelands you don't see many piles of cubed cars. What you see is far more haunting.

These are the automotive equivalents of the Paris catacombs, mass graves in orderly array, but above ground, exposed to the elements. In these yards you find rusting car cadavers piled three, five, eight high, towering columns of ex-cars leaning on each other for support. Stripped of all that's worth taking – alloys, radios, lights – all windows smashed, these are a record of our conduct. Who was taken for a ride in these? Who bought and sold them, thrashed them on the motorways? Who washed and polished them? The life cycle of an executive coupé in Britain begins under spotlights, behind plate glass in an edgelands dealership. Salesmen and saleswomen in business suits hand out brochures complete with engine spec in small print, cutaway diagrams, statistics. Interested customers sit with care on the spotless seats, stroke the steering wheel and dream. Finance is arranged, and the car leaves the edgelands for the town and suburbs. It may, of course, commute back to the edgelands every day to park outside a glass office, but many don't come back here in the early years except for annual services, tyre changes, out-of-town shopping. A few years on they may return to the dealership, outside in the rain this time, with the other used cars, and a BARGAIN sign slapped on the windscreen. Then, again, they unwind the edgelands roundabouts on their way to town. Eventually, they come back for good, a few streets down the road from where they sat in the showroom.

This time they are stripped, cannibalised, and piled high. No one minds this, no one grieves for them. No one likes to admit they love their cars so much. And seeing them treated this way is good for the soul. Or rather, it's good for the eco-soul. Surely the sight of car cadavers piled high in the rain should gladden the heart. After all, one more car on the teetering columns is one less polluter on the road. But it doesn't quite feel like that. Not to most of us, at least. It has a pathos. New cars are beautiful, and we don't like to see them reduced to this by us, by those who should have taken better care of them. And maybe, because we put so much of ourselves into our cars, maybe we see our own demise foreshadowed in theirs, our own future, cannibalised for parts, broken open, cast aside.

*

It comes as no surprise to discover that this afterlife of the automobile doesn't feature on any maps. Though these places could be factory programmed into every satnav system, with one final rhetorical flourish from the speech synthesiser's female voice, as a rush of endorphins can signal and ease our body's final letting go. *You have reached your destination.* Satnav as memento mori.

But this is to credit satnav with something approaching a mind of its own, and throughout the decade, as satnavs have become affordable and commonplace (and as the word itself entered our everyday language), we have all heard the stories of drivers failing to trust what they could see with their own eyes, marooning their articulated lorries in tiny, impassable minor roads, of drivers being led to the brink of non-existent river crossings or turning right at level crossings on to railway tracks, of drivers damaging fifteenth-century bridges or steering their fifteen-ton trucks into little cottages, even driving the wrong way along dual carriageways. Ambulances carrying human transplant organs got lost. We've heard of tourists turning up in pebble-dashed cul-de-sacs and demanding, 'Where are the waterfalls?' The village of Wedmore in Somerset asked to be wiped off the satnav grid. We have lived through the festival of satnavalia, where subservient technology has mischievously and malevolently tinkered with the demands of its human masters.

'Satnav' as an idea has taken on a life of its own and become a powerful, everyday metaphor, positioned right on a fault line between our mistrust of technology and a desire for magic and unsullied instinct. We've begun to hear satnav used as a pejorative term, way beyond the context of road travel, say, in the way an education think tank described a new generation of 'satnav students' who were incapable of thinking for themselves. We've also begun to hear it used approvingly, often when describing an 'inner satnav', the one that pigeons use to read the earth's magnetic field and plot a course for home, or that vinyl junkies deploy to track down second-hand record shops in unfamiliar towns.

*

Maps are always abstractions. The road map in particular disregards most terrain, giving the greatest visual bandwidth to blue motorways and green major roads (though train lines, in comparison, run like fine dark threads). They get us from A to B, and in so doing, distort all scale in favour of the public highway. They turn us into vectors. In the A–Zs of major English cities, there are always pages where the circuitry of streets gives way to blank grid squares, peppered with nameless ponds, industrial parks, nurseries and plantations.

Still, maps and cartography have long held a fascination for poets. Elizabeth Bishop wrote an early poem, called 'The Map', absorbed in the delicacies of tone and shading produced by the mapmaker: 'The names of seashore towns run out to sea' and off the edge of the land, the printer experiencing the 'same excitement / as when emotion too far exceeds its cause'. The poet Ciaran Carson has suggested a source for this fascination might be the way a map 'has to use shorthand, or symbols, or metaphor, and in this it resembles poetry'. Writers from Lewis Carroll to Jorge Luis Borges have even imagined maps with a scale of 1:1, a cartography that matches in size the region it is meant to describe: in the case of the former writer, to be found in desert regions lying in tatters like its own ruins; in the latter, too big to ever roll out and practically use. But global positioning and satnav have, in a sense, already ushered in the possibility of the virtual 1:1 map. What might this mean for our blank, in-between spaces?

Satnav is basically a map, or rather, it provides a mobile interface with a digital map, and though global positioning is controlled by the US military, map data is provided globally by two companies: Navteq (US) and Tele Atlas (Belgium). Field data capture teams are used in every country to determine the situation on the ground, and spot discrepancies, and this process of editing and updating map data is known as 'ground-truthing'. In *On Roads*, Joe Moran assigns the ground-truther the role of private eye, sent out to investigate the lie of the land:

Ground-truthers work in pairs, taking it in turns to do the driving while the other person taps on or talks to a laptop connected to a GPS device. These road detectives corroborate street names, count the number of roundabout exits, mark out dead ends and one-way streets and decide which bits of the road count as 'points of interest', from petrol stations to speed cameras. Like real private eyes, they supplement this intrepid tyrework with less glamorous hours in the office. Here they fast-forward through hours of CCTV footage, noting every road sign; cadge addresses and speed-limit listings from local councils and utility companies; scroll through databases of road construction companies to get advance notice of new roads; and zoom in on Google Earth to look for road markings and bits of tyre left on the road at intersections, to work out turn restrictions.

Fancying ourselves as engaged in risky ground-truthing work, we imagine we are developing a system called edgenav, a means of guiding travellers away from the speed and vector of conventional satnav travel, and a handy companion to the book we are writing. Edgenav could feature a facility for identifying the shipping container, deep in the middle of England, via information sharing with shipping companies; drivers could be alerted to long-standing graffiti on bridge overhangs or piers just as easily as to an upcoming speed camera; routes away from the main arterial roads and the floating blue band of the motorway could lead drivers into seldom visited wastelands bypassed by the flows of commerce and leisure, the landfill sites and blank unnamed pools of dark standing water. But far more importantly, edgenav could link travellers with the stories of these unseen places blurring in their peripheral vision, narrating the hidden paths and dens, the allotments and sewage farms, tapping in to the collective consciousness by using the wiki to gather and make available their human history, criss-crossing the unexamined routes and semi-urban myths and the flight paths of migrating birds.

Who would provide the all-important voice for edgenav? Celebrity sounds utterly wrong. Estuary English? Another synthetic schoolmistress? What we imagine hearing instead are many voices, the voices of den-builders and twitchers and graffiti artists and weather-station keepers. We hear something like the field recordings linguists make in schoolyards and city streets, the anonymous voices of people who still carry the traces of local places in their mouths, on their tongues, fading in and out of reception like local FM stations on a long drive.

*

Although in-car navigation has been around for a long time, perhaps satnav is still in its infancy; its potential to guide and instruct, but also to unlock the textures of the landscape we pass through only yet hinted at. Perhaps we are all early adopters of a technology that could intersect with a myriad of personal accounts and stories. All the abstractions of the Cartesian map could be enlivened, in every cultural sense. As each invisible isogloss is crossed on the long journey northwards up the M6, we could hear a voice alert the traveller: for example, the great 'trap-bath split' that runs from the Wash to the Welsh Borders. We have lost our ability to find our way using the sun, the stars, the moon, the weather, or water, plants and animals. But most of us lost it many generations ago. In some ways, we could attempt to make the world navigable this way again, and many of us fantasise about our lost masteries and resourcefulness; but the world has changed, and most of us live surrounded by mysterious labyrinths of our own making that we seem unable or unwilling to look into.

*

The roads of edgelands are the domain of business travellers by day, and boy racers by night, but there is a third set of drivers with a claim on the place. Between the hours of afternoon and evening, when the office workers have unwound the roundabouts home to the suburbs, the learner drivers head for the business parks.

Out here, there is relative calm, and the place is laid out like a model town, a microcosm of urban driving, complete with junctions, road signs, traffic lights and multiple left and right turns. Vast, empty car parks are a fine place to fine-tune your reverse-parking skills.

Between the hours of six and eight on a summer's evening, driving seems easy here. With no cyclists or pedestrians, the only danger is the chance of meeting another learner coming the wrong way round a roundabout. Good job you know how to perform an emergency stop.

*

One of the strangest encounters we had in the edgelands was following a visit to a breaker's yard on an industrial estate near Morecambe. The gates were shackled and padlocked up. We spent a while looking through a wire fence at the silent heaps of dark metal, trying to make out individual makes and models, before giving up. We were losing the light, and it was beginning to grow chilly. A dog we couldn't see was barking somewhere close by as we made our way back to the entrance of the estate. We found a man standing by his car looking into the evening sky with binoculars. The sky to the west was still a bright indigo, touched with reds and turquoises, the last embers of a typically spectacular west-coast sunset. But this man wasn't interested in sunsets. Or birds.

He had come to watch for an Iridium flare. Iridium satellites are a constellation of relatively small communications satellites, set in low earth orbit for over a decade. They have highly reflective, silver-coated panels that can catch the sun's light, producing a reflection tens of kilometres wide at the earth's surface, and, if you're standing in the right place, they are often easily visible. And now it's not even a case of being in the right place at the right time. Flare prediction programs have been designed, and it's become possible to purchase an iPhone application that works out time, altitude and azimuth relative to the phone-user's position.

As we waited – he assured us that this flare would be easily visible to the naked eye – we wondered about this as a new form of pagan moon worship, satellite idolatry, looking to the heavens to acknowledge the presence of our telecoms gods. Then it happened. At first, there's a slow and languorous brightening, and we became aware we were tracking an object. Its magnitude intensifies, flashing suddenly into brilliance for a moment, before fading away. The whole thing only lasted a few seconds, but at its brightest the satellite did seem to shine more brilliantly than Venus, the morning and evening star. It has a correspondence with those slow magnesium flares sometimes seen from a plane, when a greenhouse or pool or windscreen seems to signal back to us, and us alone, from the earth miles below; the hothouse that 'flashed uniquely' in Philip Larkin's poem 'The Whitsun Weddings'.

*

We had to go back to our notes and check whether our encounter with the Iridium watcher had taken place on 10 February 2009 at 1656 GMT (it hadn't). Because we later discovered that this was the moment one satellite, Iridium 33, had collided with a retired Russian orbiter, Kosmos 2251. This was a fairly momentous occasion, because in the fifty years humans have been launching objects into space, this marked the first time two intact spacecraft had hit each other at hypervelocity while orbiting earth. Most satellites travel at speeds ranging from 3.1 kilometres per second to 7.8 kilometres per second, so impacts cause massive disintegration: about 100,000 new pieces of debris larger than a centimetre across were dispersed in low earth orbit following the Iridium 33 collision. There was a 70 per cent increase in debris at 570 kilometres, the height of the Hubble space telescope.

As more and more of us have become dependent on GPS satellites for communications and navigation, so the orbital debris population has grown. Objects in the 1 to 10 centimetre size range are causing most concern, because they are the most dangerous, and known as the 'lethal population' (objects larger than 10 centimetres, which can be tracked, are known as the 'catalogued population'; objects smaller than 1 centimetre are called the 'risk population'): too small to reliably track, but large enough to cause massive damage if they were to hit a working satellite. It's estimated that collisions between working satellites and pieces of lethal debris will occur, on average, once every two to three years over the coming decade. The irony could be put on show at White Cube: our reliance on satnav to get us where we want to go on earth is creating a demolition derby in the skies above us, where nobody really understands the rules of the road and the impossible-to-track vehicles, while they are much smaller than the average family saloon, are travelling very, very fast.

Edgenav seems to enjoy telling all this to its driver. It's using its HAL 9000 voice to describe how fifty years' worth of scrap is zipping through the edgelands above us. The driver imagines having to dodge the carburettors of Austin Maxis and Hillman Imps, the big ends of Bedford vans and Ford Anglias, the slivers and shrapnel of unidentifiable, long-dismembered vehicles, as they make their way out of the business park and rejoin the morning rush hour. *Relax, it's only hail.* Of such stuff are edgelands nightmares made.

Paths

Planners love telling us which way to walk. Our built environment – especially our mercantile spaces, shopping centres and the like – is carefully constructed to control footflow and footfall. But we do like to collectively, unconsciously defy them. This is why we see desire paths in our landscape. Desire paths are lines of footfall worn into the ground, tracks of use. They are frowned upon in our national parkland, where they are seen as scars and deviations. PLEASE KEEP TO THE FOOTPATH. You often see desire paths in public gardens and greened city spaces, taking paved paths 'off road' into new trajectories, along roadsides and riverbanks. Our edgelands are full of them.

The post-war overspill developments seen on the edges of many of our cities were planned right down to every concrete walkway, subway and pathway. But their green squares and verges were soon criss-crossed with desire paths: a record of collective short-cuttings. In the winter, they turned to sludgy scars that spattered trousers and skirts and clung to shoes, and during hot summers they turned dusty and parched. Once established, they fell into constant use, footpaths which have never entered the literature. These footpaths of least resistance offer their own subtle resistance to the dead hand of the planner. They lead across borders, into open fields and woodland, along drainage brooks, away from the backs of the houses. On a housing estate, a path leading through a hole in a fence is still freighted with possibility. Each one offers promise and danger, whether what lies ahead is known or unknown. Each one has a flavour and mood (or several moods) all of its own.

Desire paths are interesting because of the way they come into being: a 'bottom up' system against the 'top down' methodology of the planner, and proof of human unpredictability. Nobody decides to make a desire path. There is no ribbon-cutting. These are the kinds of paths that begin over time, imperceptibly, gathering definition as people slowly recognise and legitimise the footfall of their peers. Paths are as old as the earliest transhumance, as the first drovers and movers of livestock, or even older. It might seem far-fetched to compare them to the dreaming tracks or songlines of the Australian aboriginals, but this slow erosion is how many of our roads began, navigating the easiest or best-disposed route between origin and destination on foot.

*

It is early in Easter week. Driving through some of our favourite Mancunian edgelands we see a young man, in his twenties, carrying a Cross at the side of the road. He walks quickly, but not easily. The Cross is large enough to hold a man, and the crossbeam rests on his shoulder, with his hands keeping it in place. On the foot of the Cross is a small wheel, like a stabiliser from a child's first bicycle. Apart from the weight on his shoulder, he is having trouble with the edgelands terrain. There is no pavement here, so he walks at the side of the road until a car like ours comes past, then he struggles along the grass and grit verge. When the road runs out, he carries his Cross over a stile and heads out on an edgelands path.

Spaced out behind him, at regular intervals, we pass four other men. They must be on their way from town to town, city to city, doing shifts with the Cross, then walking behind to rest their shoulders. This is an act of Easter witness, and on the streets of Manchester or Liverpool, in the shadow of towering, blackened Victorian buildings they will cut a dramatic picture. Kids will walk alongside, jeering and asking questions, old men smoking outside pubs will raise a glass and make a joke, and these are the scenes the Cross-bearers will welcome. But here in the edgelands, they look strangely isolated. Apart from the occasional car like ours, their act of witness has turned into an act of unobserved endurance.

What keeps them going through the edgelands? The lure of their destination? It should be more than that, because the Crucifixion was essentially an edgelands story. The Bible suggests that the site of the Crucifixion was 'outside the city wall', and historians now believe that the Romans favoured such 'edgelands' as their place of execution. Golgotha, it seems, was more than likely a place with two uses – working quarry and city rubbish dump. The Via Dolorosa is an edgelands path.

*

Today's edgelands Cross-bearers are followers not just of Jesus but of Arthur Blessitt. At five o'clock one morning in 1969, this devout café proprietor heard the voice of God calling him to take down the twelve-foot cross from the wall of his café on Hollywood's Sunset Boulevard and walk the highways of the world. Over forty years and 38,000 miles later he is still going. He has carried his Cross through warzone, wasteland and wilderness. He even has an entry in the *Guinness Book of Records* for the world's longest walk, and for walking the greatest documented lifetime mileage.

Blessitt's official website includes detailed instructions on how to make your own full-sized Cross, including how to construct it for easy dismantling at airports, and how to choose the correct wheel to maximise your mileage. He began his walk without a wheel, but the weight of the Cross dragging on the road shaved an inch per day off the wood. Among the many interesting facts about Arthur Blessitt's epic walk (including his worst meal, which was rat soup in Belize) is the following:

'The Cross has been turned away from being left overnight at more than half the churches requested, but has never been turned away from spending the night at a bar or nightclub in forty years around the world.'

*

We know that an unseen, untouched English landscape is a myth. We know that a long and complex interaction between constant natural processes and more recent human activity has largely formed all the landscapes we can see today, and that landscape is indivisible from the human world. The word 'landscape' itself found its way into English from the Dutch word 'landschap', which meant an area, a tract, a unit of jurisdiction, and was originally carried across the wide barrier of the North Sea by sixteenth-century Dutch artists. From its etymological beginnings in English, landscape has been very much a part of human culture: something that includes nature, rather than something that is wholly consistent of it.

Landscaping, used as a verb, perhaps makes this explicit, but also excavates a paradox in the word: when we landscape something these days, what we are in effect trying to do most often is disguise the physical facts of raw human activity, to cover our tracks, to conceal by camouflaging the terrain according to some orderly idea of 'the natural'.

*

Although many of the tiny branch capillaries on Dr Richard Beeching's list were underused, and the age of the car was just dawning, the prevailing view – half a century later – is that the Beeching railway cuts were an unnecessary and short-sighted act of national vandalism. Laments were written in song, by the likes of Flanagan & Allen and Flanders & Swann, whose 'Slow Train' managed to conflate station names to make them sound even more rustic and elegiac: 'Formby Four Crosses', 'Armley Moor Arram'. By the mid-Nineties we were feeling so nostalgic about our lost branch lines that we gave them their own TV sitcom – *Oh Doctor Beeching* – which painted a rosy picture of a pre-axe country station threatened with closure.

Edward Thomas' 'Adelstrop' – written in 1914 – describes an unscheduled stop at a small Gloucestershire station on an Oxford to Worcester train. This famous lyric evokes a moment of aware-ness, peace and beauty as the poet hears 'all the birds of Oxfordshire and Gloucestershire', and (like many of Thomas' poems) it has an elegiac air, deepened by the knowledge that Thomas himself was killed in the First World War. Visitors to Adelstrop today can read the poem on a plaque in the village bus shelter. The railway station was axed in 1966. For many readers, the poem has another elegiac undertow – the sense that Thomas' moment of awareness is no longer possible, in an age where trains no longer go down sleepy branch lines, nor stop at sunlit halts with proudly tended baskets full of blooms.

But there is a counterweight to all this pre-Beeching nostalgia, and the edgelands are the chief beneficiaries. Some of the 10,000 miles of ex-railway line is now unrecognisable, filled in and built upon. But many of them still bear the form and sweep of the old lines, and this has offered them an afterlife as extended pathways (sometimes billed as 'linear parks') for walkers and cyclists. South-east of Manchester, between Marple and Macclesfield, the Middlewood Way traces the path of a former branch line closed in 1970, snaking alongside the Macclesfield Canal as it passes former silk mills turned into luxury apartments, under bridges and over viaducts, overlooked by the backs of factories and farms.

Like many of these 'linear parks', the Middlewood Way has hot and cold spells. Quiet for much of the day, it comes into its own at dawn when the joggers, dog-walkers and cycle commuters emerge. The formerly close-cropped embankments have been allowed to flourish, so long stretches of the Way are shady, secluded, soundproofed from the nearby roads. This makes it a popular bolt-hole for office workers on weekday lunchtimes, stepping out from their software start-ups in the converted mills to take stock, have a smoke, make a call about a job advert, start an office affair.

In the former cotton town of Bollington, on the Middlewood Way between Macclesfield and Marple, the residents have raised funding for a gritstone labyrinth, set at the side of the track where the town's railway station once stood, before the Beeching axe felled it. A photograph in the local visitor centre shows a Bollington family a century ago, waiting at the station to begin their journey to a new life in Canada. Now the station is a labyrinth, the travellers are stressed and bemused office workers, and the journey is within.

*

Even our motorways were footpaths briefly before their unceasing roar was switched on. Many children growing up in the Sixties and Seventies had the chance to walk along them, as different sections were being constructed. It was exciting to stroll, three of you abreast, each with a lane to yourself, along miles of empty virgin tarmac, reading the huge blue signs for junctions that took long minutes to loom up and pass by; which, in the adult life to come, would pass through the field of vision and recede into a rear-view mirror in seconds.

Yet it's difficult to imagine abandoned roads. After Dr Beeching's rationalisation of the rail network in the Sixties, we're used to walking along ghostly dismantled railways, changed into footpaths or cycle paths, reclaimed foot corridors passing straight through the landscape. Roads are different. As Black Box Recorder put it, describing the English motorway system, 'it's been there forever, it's never going to change'. Our road network is a living system, a work-in-progress, the gradual result of many centuries of adaptation since the first prehistoric trackways were established. Even though the rate of road-building accelerated in the last century, our network today still bears many resemblances to the slower models used by Roman legions, medieval traders and the first Royal Mail coaches. Still, there will come a general slowing down. We try to picture – in the post-petrol era – being able to walk the M1 Way, from Brent Cross to Scotch Corner, leaving the gravitational pull of London and its inner planet, the M25, on foot, staying overnight at service stations reconverted into hostels. We mean, actually walk it; not use it as a loose narrative device for some *flâneurisms*.

*

There is a world of difference between walking a path and a road. The bigger roads discourage foot traffic, and motorways make it illegal except in an emergency. Our smaller roads have long since been hijacked by the motor car, and even those roads, demoted by newer, bigger carriageways, orphaned and bypassed, can turn to sudden spate on weekday mornings and evenings: the rat run. The roadside walker feels constantly pushed to the margins, ever vigilant and wary.

The landscape passes slowly, but it's difficult to relax and feel a part of it. Paths, on the other hand, put the walker back into the centre of things.

Even our longest, official rambles can offer good edgelands walking. The Dales Way stretches eighty-four miles from Ilkley in the West Riding to the shores of Lake Windermere at Bowness, and is mostly what you'd expect: limestone hills and lonely moors, deep wooded valleys like the Strid, ancient ruins like Bolton Abbey, churches with lych gates, little tourist honeypots cluttered with tea rooms and outdoor-clothing emporiums. Even so, the first few miles of path following the River Wharfe can't make up its mind, and you find yourself passing under concrete subways, along back roads in view of roundabout islands, past caravan parks and garden centres, before it finally begins to relax into tranquil wilderness (though never too far from scones or vernacular ale).

*

We meet in Carlisle on a summer morning, to pick up a path that follows the course of the River Caldew out through the city centre and into its hinterlands. Past the gasworks, past three-quarter-empty marshalling and lorry yards padlocked off from the road, to a point where we drop down alongside the river, into a leafy dark. The overgrowth is at its annual thickest and most assertive, and at certain points we walk single file along the reddish, sandy track, arms raised above the nettles and brambles like jungle soldiers fording an invisible river. We soon tune in to the rhythms of the path, the ground underfoot, its sidelong detours leading down the bank to the river's edge, the litter and traces of people who have been here to drink, unseen from the road.

The Caldew was an industrial river, powering the textile plants that flourished alongside it for two centuries. From the weir above Ferguson Mill, some of the older red-stoned buildings still stand on the opposite bank, converted into housing now. But there is the Pirelli plant, a grey box on the hillside, and soon we pass close by the Stead McAlpine print and dye works: the warm air suddenly smells of burning paper. Here, the path's sideshoots allow us to clamber down on to gravel banks where the river has slowed to a backwater overhung by ash and elder. A small cairn supports a Y-shaped stick, a rod rest, though the angler is nowhere to be seen. A heron watches us, furiously. Further upstream, sand martins have colonised the banks, burrowing in to the soft red earth, their nesting places a little altered and eroded every time they return in the spring. A grey mains pipe crosses the river on its own metal bridge. It's caged off, and defensive, but the graffiti and the gap in its railings reveal that this is a favourite spot for children and teenagers.

The land widens out, and now the pitch of the path becomes airier. Power lines cross broad meadows left to grow wild and full of their own insect electric noise. Up ahead lies the Nestlé factory: we're told that these fields once contained sprinklers and jets that would squirt some kind of junket or dairy by-product into the air. After we've passed the fenced-off, tidy lawns of the factory, and reached the village of Dalston, miles of rich agricultural land lie ahead of us, then the Lake District, and dark Skiddaw, where the Caldew rises. We leave the unexpected, hidden landscape and move into the countryside.

*

In The English Path Kim Taplin explored the path in literature and the 'mental landscapes' that grew out of paths. She wondered how paths themselves shifted in and out of favour as a fit subject for

writers. The eighteenth century was a bad time for paths in literature, as if their very ordinariness and down-to-earthness somehow
barred them from writerly attention. This is from the Quaker poet
John Scott of Amwell's *The Amoebean Eclogues*, written in the 1780s:

> In shady lanes the foxglove bells appear,
> And golden spikes the downy mulleins rear;
> The enclosure ditch luxuriant mallows hide;
> And branchy succory crowds the pathway wide.

Taplin picks up on a telling image here, that 'enclosure ditch', which
seems to anticipate John Clare by a few decades; John Hoole, a friend
and admirer of Scott's work, might have struggled with what Taplin
calls the 'shameless modernism' of such an image. It could have
been exactly what Hoole had in mind when he described his unease
with 'such names and circumstances, as, in my opinion, no versifi-
cation, however harmonious, can make poetical'. How would he have
coped with barbed-wire fencing or the IKEA car park?

*

There is something about a path through trees that captures our
imaginations. Maybe it goes back to folk tales of children walking
through forests, being told not to stray from the path. But, of course,
they do stray from the path, and that is why we need folk tales.

We take the metaphors for our lives from the language we inherit,
but we shape and colour them from our own experience. 'Life is a
journey' is such a pervasive metaphor that it has long deserved its place
in the 'Dictionary of Clichés'. But the wealth of metaphors-for-life that
cluster round it suggest that we have not tired of it yet: 'roller-coaster
ride', 'uphill struggle', 'free-wheeling' . . .

But of all the metaphors in the 'life-is-a-journey' suite, perhaps the most interesting is 'path': 'this is my chosen path', 'the path to righteousness', 'pathfinders'. As a rule, nobody talks about a spiritual journey as a highway or cruise. If you are going to get spiritual, you really need a path to walk, preferably through trees to add a brooding atmosphere. Where would yours be? An Alpine edge, perhaps? Or one that snakes through New York's Central Park when all the blooms are full?

Well, our spiritual path would be a track worn down by dog-walkers and schoolkids, on the outskirts of a north-west English conurbation. It would start on scrappy grass, then weave its way through a copse of feral trees. Every now and then a makeshift den or tree house can be seen, or a water tower looming where the trees peter out. Charred bonfire patches crop up on one side or the other, and the sky is overcast above.

But do be careful out there. Sometimes there are two paths, and you have to choose. The poet Robert Frost famously set out the problem, describing a parting of the ways as he walked in the woods. Realising that he couldn't take both paths, he stood and gazed down one enticing avenue as far as he could see:

> Then took the other, as just as fair,
> And having perhaps the better claim,
> Because it was grassy and wanted wear.

Our edgelands spiritual path may not be as romantic as some, but perhaps it is 'the one less travelled by', and as the Frost poem reminds us, if we take that path it can make 'all the difference'.

*

There are landscape artists currently at work for whom edgelands are important, who have especially recognised the mystery and allure of a path. David Rayson's paintings in the series *From Ashmore Park to Wednesfield* lead us along a canal path, past dens, the Devil's Elbow, the null grey Linthouse Bridge, in the West Midlands where he grew up. There are no people about, just their traces in the old leaden water, the missing railing, the litter, all linked by the implacable path. It follows the backs of houses, and passes under a busier road (whose lamp tops we can just see), suggesting that this is a private, forgotten route, bypassed by the world as it speeds up.

Another Midlander, George Shaw, paints the Tile Hill suburb where he grew up using Humbrol enamels familiar to anybody whose eyes have ever watered in the fumy business of building an Airfix kit model. Again, this is the absolutely overlooked ordinary, accorded the attention of the artist; the late Gordon Burn once commented upon this sense of project and intensity, 'painting the back of the social club in Tile Hill with all the seriousness of Monet painting Rouen Cathedral'. Shaw's *Twelve Short Walks*, printed in dust grain gravure, again take us round the backs of the houses, through patches of woodland and bramble poking through the railings; again, so utterly deserted that the path itself becomes an absence, luminous, compelling. Both artists work largely from memory.

*

Bidston Moss on the Wirral must be one of the most worked-over, altered, *landscaped* areas of landscape in the country. It lies just inland of the Mersey and the sea, near the northernmost tip of the peninsula at Wallasey, a blank zone on the map criss-crossed by railway lines, the Mersey Tunnel approach roads and the M53 motorway.

Within this zone, you find a network of paths. We entered into it by means of a tiny one at the back of the B&Q car park, leading through a gate in the dull, metal-spiked railings into a dark waste ground beneath the flyovers, greeted by undergrowth festooned with a spectacular array of moulded plastics: it seemed as if every colour and variety of polyethylene, polypropylene, polystyrene and polyvinyl has landed up here, snarled in the low scrubland and grasses, thrown from the roads overhead or blown from the loading bays to the rear of the superstores. It's a huge litter trap, an open space surrounded by people passing through very quickly, an un-acknowledged or quickly disregarded blindspot. Looking closer, you can see how trefoils and bindweeds have begun to grow back over some of the takeaway cartons and soft-drinks bottles.

Bidston Moss has always lacked definition, always been off-radar. It was formerly a low-lying, marshy inlet, drained and reclaimed in the second half of the nineteenth century. Before then, the coastline here was the haunt of wreckers – the mouth of the Mersey was once one of the busiest shipping lanes in the world – and outlaw gangs worked the dunes and beaches, lighting beacons to draw ships on to the banks at Wallasey and Mockbeggar Sands, and carrying their spoils inland through secret paths across what was then the deep and impenetrable boggy region around Bidston. Intimate knowledge of these paths made all the difference: this was a life-and-death business.

Once the area was drained, it was used as grazing land for a while until the Thirties, when it became a landfill and tipping site for domestic, commercial and industrial waste. The mound that built up over the decades became visible from miles away across the water in Liverpool, a hundred-foot-high landmark of rubbish. And then a new kind of salvager appeared. Tip scavengers – or 'totters' – began to work the site, sifting through the wreckage looking for anything of value. The site took in a huge amount of building materials, and a trade began in scrap-metal cabling and wiring, the plastic insulating sheath burned away in tip fires. Copper and lead were best, trundled off to the scrap dealers in a Kwik Save trolley. This was Merseyside's economic nadir, and people were desperate. They were an image from antiquity, or the developing world, the grimy faced rag-picker and bone-collector. There is a photograph of a totter, taken by Peter Marlowe in April 1985. Marlowe's tip scavenger is cowled and furtive, a character from the Middle Ages; Brueghel meets Magnum Photo Agency.

There were still scavengers on Bidston Moss as late as the mid-Nineties, working alongside the seagulls, hardcore recyclers. Merseyside Waste Disposal began employing security guards and dogs, but it was the closure of the tip that did for them. In recent years the site has undergone a process of restoration work. A green and largely open space of meadows and woodland has been carefully established by degrees; phases on a planning document. On the ground, paper-mill sludge and sewage cake from Ellesmere Port have prepared a new surface, which in turn has been planted with grasses and herbs and saplings. But 'restoration' here doesn't mean an attempt to recreate the original, treacherous marshland that once obtained here: what it has created is a very twenty-first-century melange of low scrubby woods, footpaths and cycle paths, graffitoed bridges and finger posts, pylons and road pillars. Even here, where recent planning has proscribed pathways for all kinds of public use, desire paths are already worn into the earth, cutting off corners, creating short cuts, circuits within circuits. The unplannable edgelands, reasserting themselves.

Dens

Is den-building a lost art? A generation or two ago, our edgelands were full of these most private and local of constructions, which have more in common with badger setts or fox lairs than any human habitation, usually hidden in waste ground or railway cuttings or shelterbelts of thin woodland on the edge of newly developed housing. Picture some typical scenes . . .

Inside a large ditch overhung with whitethorn that marks the border between a few acres of unkempt meadow and the perimeter of a private golf course, a tepee-like vertical frame has been attempted using pliant elder branches, which in turn have been cross-woven then packed with grasses to disguise its presence; the floor inside has been carpeted with an off cut of ratty Axminster and the rubberised foot mats from an abandoned car; a red plastic milk crate, partially melted in one corner from the heat of a fire, serves as both chair and table, where a boy is studying a punished copy of *Mayfair*, pulled from a hedge full of empty vodka bottles in a lay-by.

A sheet of tarpaulin, stolen from a nearby lorry yard, has been used to insulate the inside of another hollow bramble hedge near a main road; the entry point is a crawlspace a few feet lower, hidden on the leeward side, and only the slimmest child can enter, beaver-like, into its hidden space; a hole has been left in the crown of the construction to act as a chimney for the small fires that will kipper the clothes and hair of its occupants with woodsmoke; a few broken-down Golden Wonder cardboard boxes make a comfortable if slightly damp and spongy floor, where a boy has stripped down the spring-piston mechanism of a .22 air pistol.

An underground labyrinth, dug into the soft earth of a back field covered in great stands of nettles, its passageways expertly shored up with broken crating, panels knocked out of old chests of drawers and branches, all converging on a central chamber lined with dried grass and old lino, like a scaled-down re-enactment of a Western Front dugout, where a boy is carefully filling a milk bottle with siphoned petrol.

*

The den is a secret place, built outside the confines of the adult world. It is a place of retreat, but also a place of togetherness, a social space, that reinforces allegiances and bonds between small groups or gangs. Children have always built them instinctively, but could it be that the English post-war edgelands saw a Golden Age of den-building? Children were widely encouraged to get out from under parents' feet and play outdoors without too great a perceived fear of danger from predatory adults, and this coincided with shifts in social housing policy, the clearance of inner-city dwellings and the construction of huge new housing-estate developments, often on the urban periphery. All of a sudden it wasn't just Peter and Jane from the Ladybird Key Words Reading Scheme who could play with tents in a greenscape of seemingly infinite resource; used to city housing with small backyards and streets to play in, children found themselves on the edge of what seemed a prairie-vast wilderness, often littered with the detritus left behind after their new houses had been built.

It was paradise. In summer, time at home indoors contracted to sleeping, and occasional visits for food. The edgelands provided a space of abandonment out of the watchful eye of the adult world, and also provided all of the terrain and materials a child's imagination needed to physically make its own world and reinforce a new sense of itself.

*

A tree house is the ultimate den. To succeed, it must be inaccessible to adults once the rope ladder is pulled up, hidden high in the canopy like a rook's nest.

From Dennis the Menace to Bart Simpson, childhood's HQ is located in a small makeshift covered platform on the bough of a sturdy tree, like an elevated shed. The standard model has four wooden walls with narrow window holes, a waterproof roof and a trapdoor in the floor to permit, or repel, visitors. The best of them are not built in a scrawny backyard tree by your dad, but built by you and your mates with 'borrowed' tools in an overgrown oak in the edgelands. This, of course, raises other issues. If it's not in your garden, a tree house must be well hidden and defensible.

This is tree house as castle, fortress. Edgelands tree houses, like any edgelands den, can change hands, can be kicked to matchwood by other kids, or taken over as their own, padlocked and painted with their own KEEP OUT warnings. But with any good tree house, as with any hill fort, the incumbent has a key advantage – height. Peering through your arrow-slit windows, you get early warning of potential invaders from every angle. And besides, the view from up there is fantastic.

In Kathleen Jamie's poem 'The Tree House' another ascent takes place, into the trees and back to childhood, and that sense of a unique vista is vividly expressed:

> Hands on a low limb, I braced,
> swung my feet loose, hoisted higher,
> heard the town hall clock toll, a car
> breenge home from a club
> as I stooped inside. Here

> I was unseeable. A bletted fruit
> hung through tangled branches
> just out of reach. Over house roofs:
> sullen hills, the firth drained
> down to sandbanks: the *Reckit Lady*, the *Shair as Daith*.

*

Den-building was usually a summer activity: that border ditch could flood with rainwater or agricultural run-off come autumn; no amount of tarpaulin could withstand a winter gale. One exception to this rule, though, was the bonfire den.

Growing up on an estate, it was as if a chemical reaction in the pineal glands of its children – triggered by shortening daylight, the earthy smell of the first winter vegetables and conker-fall – sent them looking for wood. Timber in all its forms, in fact anything combustible, foraged from the edgelands, where sheets of plywood were lifted from the yellow grass like piano lids, then carried a corner each, abandoned cable drums wheeled easily away, all manner of posts and planks and fencing uprooted and worked free, all of it brought by any means to the pre-ordained site of the fire, and slowly and carefully built around the central axis of a telegraph pole or tree stump.

Then followed days and nights of escalating tension. As the

bonfire took its rickety conical shape, it became vulnerable: kids from rival streets or estates would have desperately liked to steal some of its timber, or, worse still, set light to it a day or two early and dance triumphantly around its flames. And so the larger bonfires would factor in a hollow, a space that could be occupied so the entire construction could be guarded. Being inside one of these spaces, lit by the flame of a carefully managed candle, one imagines wooden pyramids, wigwams, sockets of antiquity with the craziest wooden panelling. Simon Armitage's bonfire poem 'Five Eleven Ninety Nine' delineates these temporary dens: 'priest-holes, passageways, / a box-room, alcoves, doors.' Of all the kinds of den, these were the shortest-lived, and it was an honour to be invited into their fastnesses to keep watch.

*

Stolen vehicles often still find their ways into the edgelands, joyridden and driven off the road to be burnt out and abandoned in fields and ditches like used pornography. Cars and vans provide another species of den, a space where children can turn immobility into limitless freedoms simply through exercising the force of an undisturbed imagination. In Geoffrey Hill's *Mercian Hymns*, a magnificent conflation of English myth and memory with the edgelands, the child Offa understands the pleasures of such hermitic and lonely journeying:

> After school, he lured Ceolred, who was sniggering with fright, down to the old quarries, and flayed him. Then, leaving Ceolred, he journeyed for hours, calm and alone, in his private derelict sandlorry named Albion.

This is deep edgelands, in the way Hill's 'verset' suggests the constancy of our creaturely need to secrete ourselves in the landscape. It might also remind us of the landscape before it was Romanticised; how any littered clearing with the charred remains of a fire in a denuded patch of roadside woodland can find its echo in the utilitarian coppices of thirteen centuries ago.

*

Despite the relative freedoms that such landscapes afforded the child den-builder, part of the unspoken contract of dens includes elements of danger, as if the nest-like space is all the more cosy and secure for having some darkness or threat it needs to keep out. Any private land abutting edgelands creates a sense of unease and uncertainty for the den-builders who have chosen to occupy it, like a robin that builds its nest in a car engine or drainpipe, or the stone curlew, which often chooses to lay its eggs and rear its young on the precarious floors of working gravel quarries. Golf-course green-keepers become figures of fear. The low diesel thrum of a farmer's tractor means the code word for *Abort!* is deployed and a secret plan put into hasty action. Dens are also sites of territorial conflict between the children of rival areas, reinforcing the sense of edge-lands being a kind of no-man's-land.

*

In recent years, den-building has received something of an official imprimatur, part of a general recognition that we all live in medi-ated bubbles and have forgotten what it's like to get messy with nature. 'Nature' here becomes a place of team-building and activ-ities, preferably in a National Park, designed to throw us back on our innate resourcefulness and predilection for working 'as part of a group'. Before children lose their way and learn how to steal efficiently, or develop ruinous substance dependencies, and thus secure their places on abseiling and canoeing courses, den-building is to be made safe for them.

In 2006 the Forestry Commission issued a booklet titled 'Rope Swings, Dens, Treehouses and Fires', which carried the detumescent subtitle 'A risk-based approach for managers facilitating self-built play structures and activities in woodland settings'. A tree house is 'a den on legs'. The booklet correlates den-construction and den location and use into levels of 'low risk', 'medium risk' and 'high risk'. On this scale, 'low risk' means dens built from natural materials, 'such as branches, bracken, leaves and other vegetation', while the use of pallets, old kitchen units or, worse still, metals and asbestos and cars, together with tunnelling and deep excavations, takes the den into the 'high risk' category. Edgelands dens would typically fail these building regs, being of necessity a bricolage of available natural materials and human waste. Reading this booklet, you realise how far we have come from public information films warning of the dangers of children entombing themselves in fly-tipped refrigerators on waste ground. You also realise how separate our official countryside is from our edgelands.

And the distance travelled between children and adults. Adults need to be especially resourceful in order to recreate the kind of spaces of solitude and apartness from the world that once seemed to come so easily, another reason why the great unwritten history of childhood den-building is particularly precious and important.

*

This commodification and sanitisation of den-building by adults has spread to the tree house too. Like the pirate ship and the castle,

43

the tree house is one of the oft-repeated tropes of play spaces designed by adults for children, or (perhaps more honestly) by adults for themselves.

On the outskirts of Alnwick, Northumberland, is one of Britain's favourite visitor attractions. Alnwick Castle is now perhaps best known for its role as various parts of Hogwarts in the Harry Potter films. But the real attraction for many is the garden. Here, amid spectacular water features and a dizzying array of exotic plants, is one of the world's biggest tree houses.

Constructed out of cedar, redwood and pine – all, naturally, from sustainable sources – the Alnwick garden tree house is in fact a tree mansion, or perhaps a tree hamlet. Strung between the boughs of a towering lime copse, this is what grown-ups do when they get the time and money to create the tree house they dreamt about in childhood.

Up here in the canopy, there are restaurants with log fires (chilling in thought, but warming in reality) and bars, shops and classrooms with video screens. This is a multi-storey, multi-platform, multi-tasking tree house, and it is an utterly fantastic piece of work. But, but . . .

It is only when you cross the rope bridges between the trees that you can feel a rush of vertigo. Although you are – as always in this tree house – perfectly safe, you do feel the bridge sway and wobble under your feet. You do reach for the guide ropes to help you safely across. You do look down at the visitors on the path below, and take a deep breath as they smile up at you. This is one of the world's greatest, as well as biggest, tree houses, but it lacks – let's face it – edge. A true tree house is a bodge job, complete with loose boards, protruding nail heads, dodgy ropes and a powerful smell of creosote.

*

There were always indoor dens too, temporary structures based on clothes racks, kitchen tables or under-stairs cupboards. But perhaps most dens have moved indoors now. In an age of over-protective parenting and health and safety zealotry, we are often told that children have lost the right to roam. Whereas their parents might have vanished for a whole day in the summer, only returning when the light was at its thinnest, now children – we are told by shrill columnists – are driven to one another's houses for carefully moderated play, usually on screens. This is, at most, only a partial truth. There are still places (especially those large estates on the edges of our cities) where kids come and go as they please, which provokes the ire of those same shrill columnists.

For pre-school children, the indoor den was always the haven of choice, and still is. Across Britain, on rainy mornings when CBeebies has lost its hold, parents are enlisted to help tie duvet covers to newel posts, then sofa cushions and stuffed toys complete the staircase den, and snacks and drinks are passed down through a gap in the roof.

This is all fine, until you need to get upstairs, and the den is then dismantled (not without protests), on condition that it is reassembled under the bunk bed in the child's bedroom. These indoor dens leave powerful imprints on grown-ups' memories. It is something to do with layers of security: den, bedroom, house, roof after roof of insulation from the world outside.

*

Looking for signs of twenty-first-century wild den-building as an adult only reinforces the chasms of difference between the way we learn to habitually look at and experience landscape as children. Apart from the deeply uncomfortable sense of intrusion and trespass one feels thrashing through undergrowth and stooping awkwardly into hollows and through fence gaps, especially anywhere near schools, within earshot of a classroom practising synthetic phonic reading, you are aware of how differently you see this world, how you can no longer get your eye in, or realise the imaginative potential in what you see. A clearing, an old rope swing, a few cardboard boxes turning to mulch in the rosebay willowherb, cigarette ends ... Promising signs, but even though our forays into fields and waste ground were hardly scientific and exhaustive, we didn't once find anything we could call an active den.

Still, it's possibly all still going on, somewhere out of sight of prying adult eyes, like the fantasy of hearth fires kept burning continuously for decades. Somewhere deep inside the reclaimed ground, infill and maze of paths just beyond the edges of a Sixties housing development, a den, in continuous use since the estate was built, occupied by subsequent generations of children, handed on as fit for purpose and reused like the lair of a wild animal. Even when dens surround themselves with, indeed are constructed from, the things we discard, they also seem to link us with something much older and bigger than us, and in that way their loss on our collective imagination is incalculably larger than we might expect. In Clive King's classic children's book *Stig of the Dump* from 1963, Barney is warned away from venturing too close to the chalk pit, but can't resist the allure of its rubbish-choked depths:

This had been the side of a hill once, he told himself. Men had come to dig chalk and left this huge hole in the side of the earth. He thought of all the sticks of chalk they must have made, and all the blackboards in all the schools they must have written on. They must have dug and dug for hundreds of years. And then they got tired of digging, or somebody told them to stop before they dug away the side of the hill. And now they did not know what to do with this empty hole and were trying to fill it up again. Anything people didn't want they threw into the bottom of the pit.

Containers

In part, containers made the edgelands, because they changed the way our manufacturing bases related to our ports. They dismantled an older means of production and transportation, but created a new one in the process. Places outside our larger urban centres could take advantage of cheap transportation, as containerisation changed the complexion of the entire global economy. In *The Box*, his study of the world the shipping container made, Marc Levinson put the transformation in simple, diminished, human terms: for merchant seamen, shore leave used to mean a few days carousing in the bars and shebeens of some exotic port city; suddenly, it meant instead a few hours waiting in a floodlit car park, their ship ready to weigh anchor as soon as high-speed cranes had finished loading boxes on and off its cargo decks. As The Fall's Mark E. Smith sung in 'The Container Drivers' back in 1980, in this new roll-on, roll-off world there was nothing much to look at beyond a car park and a grey port.

Smith had worked as a clerk for an importing and exporting business on Salford Docks in the mid-1970s, when the effects of containerisation were being felt keenly in places like Manchester and Liverpool, and The Fall were early appreciators and portraitists of the English edgelands: as well as 'The Container Drivers', early songs like 'Industrial Estate' and 'English Scheme', and references to bed and breakfasts in Retford and Wimpey cranes and drinkers from the slaughterhouse and motorway services suggest how familiar they were with this demi-monde.

*

Whether we make them or not, the things we want to buy still come, from places where such things are still made, and when those things come, they come to the edgelands, to be targeted at our shops and homes.

Container yards are places of beauty and mystery. Their aesthetic appeal lies partly in their uniformity – hundreds of ribbed steel boxes in a range of colours, emblazoned with Chinese characters or company names – Maersk, Hapag-Lloyd, Hanjin Shipping. They have come a long way, and they bear the scars.

Stacked high in rows across vast fields, their paint is flaking, dull, battered by the waves and winds. But all the damage is worthwhile, because inside these containers are our new things, and they are pristine in the darkness, still encased in plastic and cardboard, our sealed and unblemished toys, electronics, white goods, clothes.

*

Of course, not all containers reach us. One estimate suggests up to 10,000 containers are lost at sea each year. Some are destined to float for eternity, pulled by the currents, endangering shipping. Written-off, beyond rescue, these surreal time capsules are cut loose.

The Lakeland poet Norman Nicholson once said that when he had trouble sleeping on a night of wild weather, he would think of the small high lake called Devoke Water, one of the bleakest places in the west of the Lake District, and picture how much worse the conditions would be up there.

There is similar comfort to be drawn on sleepless nights from the thought of a canary-yellow container, riding the fiercest waves of the icy Southern Ocean, packed sardine-tight with Disco Barbies or iPod Touches. It can be oddly consoling. Unless, of course, you happen to be on a boat in the Southern Ocean.

*

Is the container, that essential image of our epoch, becoming a meme? If you look around the edgelands you might think so. Domestic storage centres offer hope to those between homes, or those with more possessions than floor space. And that solution comes in the shape of a container, anchored in a solid, watertight building. You pay your monthly fee, and for that you get a key to a numbered door. Behind that door is an empty space with dimensions to suit your monthly fee. And that space is all yours.

It cannot be living, noxious or illegal, but other than that you can keep what you like in your numbered container, for as long as you keep paying the monthly fee. Some use it as temporary storage, some as an off-board attic. Some use it as a playroom, or a hobby room. But now there's a new twist. Some of these containers are being rented out as start-up offices. Simple and cheap, they offer a place to sit, an Internet connection, a phone and a small space of your own, until your business grows and you can move in to one of the multi-occupancy office buildings in the nearby business park. Then you might get a parking space, too.

Containers as a meme? Well, it isn't just domestic storage centres. Think of budget hotels with rooms as small and bare as containers, or garden offices for the self-employed, or modular urban housing. Containers are coming to a street near you. And to the Southern Ocean.

Shipping containers once enjoyed a second life as mobile shops on housing estates. Easy to secure at night, and difficult to broach without serious cutting gear, they superseded the Luton vans or caravans propped up on bricks that had formerly been used to serve a community of a few streets and squares. Walking up the ramp, there would be a counter, which somebody had taken the trouble to hinge so that access was easy, and the smell of a paraffin heater somewhere at the back. Mostly they sold sweets to children coming and going from school, and were often plonked strategically where pathways converged near a school gate or bus stop. They sold loose cigarettes and pints of milk, too, but the sweets were the thing . . . Refreshers, gobstoppers, blackjacks, fizz bombs, sherbet dips, cola bottles, shrimps, pineapple cubes, liquorice laces, space invaders; garishly bright, sugary exotica that sweetened the greyness of a morning or the winter dark, dispensed from a metal box that arrived one day like the rectilinear anomaly in 2001: A Space Odyssey.

When we see one now, we think of them in distant, darker places, too, war zones, a kind of ubiquitous Lego used to shelter – a checkpoint on Highway One between Kabul and Kandahar in Afghanistan; the strengthened sleeping quarters of the HM Consul-General in southern Iraq, so thickly encased in concrete it can withstand a direct hit from a rocket attack – or to contain: the Camp Delta jail facilities at Guantánamo Bay were constructed out of welded shipping containers; there are stories of them being used as makeshift holding tanks elsewhere, airless, overheated, overrun with huge banana rats.

When we see one now, we exercise our imaginative X-ray vision, having seen images of backscatter X-rays at ports of entry, and we stare blankly as a long caravan of containers moves slowly through an English railway station, trying to penetrate their dull marine reds and blues and greens, punished and battered by their trans-global journeyings.

*

Nowadays, we are so accustomed to art being made from the commonplace, the everyday, that it's possible art historians in future centuries will think of the B&Q outlet and our contemporary art world in the same way as Julien 'Père' Tanguy's paint shop in Paris and the post-Impressionists. Still, artists have taken to the shipping container over the last decade with real inventiveness. Perhaps it's because the container carries a hidden charge of displacement and immigration, while at the same time being ubiquitous and unremarkable.

CABIN/ET could turn up anywhere. CABIN/ET is a recycled shipping container that has been turned into a cabinet of curiosities, mounted on ornamental iron pedestals, its interior space lined with Douglas fir and furnished: surely, Doctor Who would have used a shipping container as his Tardis, had the BBC, through some wrinkle in space-time, commissioned the series in the Noughties rather than the Sixties? It plays with our imaginative sense of what's inside these over-familiar boxes, its fine wooden interior completely at odds with its exterior, suggesting a cabin from a different age of seafaring.

Audiences turning up to see Clare Bayley's *The Container* at the Young Vic were warned that this wasn't going to be any ordinary night in the theatre, and that those of a claustrophobic disposition might like to reconsider. That was assuming they could get hold of a ticket: audiences were limited to twenty-eight, because the entire production took place inside a shipping container. We couldn't get a ticket.

A monstrous container even managed to find its way into the Turbine Hall at Tate Modern. *How It Is*, by the Polish artist Miroslaw Balka, is a huge steel box twice the size of the biggest standard container at thirty metres long, that stood on stilts in the Turbine Hall all through the freezing winter of 2009–10. A ramp invited the viewer to climb slowly up the incline to view its cargo: pitch darkness. All the resonances of climbing into a box, and of being inside such an unbearable darkness, sound clearly, but *How It Is* also felt as if some deep-space transporter of the future had arrived back on earth having harvested antimatter from a black hole.

*

When, at the beginning of the decade, the artist Michael Landy catalogued and destroyed all his worldly belongings as a piece of performance art called *Break Down* (7,227 objects, processed into over 5.75 tonnes of raw materials) it elicited a range of responses. Some were bewildered, some nonplussed, some impressed by what seemed to be an attack on our acquisitive culture. Others were more cynical. After all, how long would it take to stock up with things again?

In the Seventies and Eighties there was something of a consensus about the game we were playing: 'the one who dies with the most things wins'. Of course, you couldn't take it with you, but most people, winners and losers (however they might wish to play a different game), agreed that this was the only game in town.

As the Nineties turned into the Noughties, the nature of the game seemed less certain. If the planet itself was threatened by some aspects of the old game, then maybe we needed a new one.

Of course, the new game hasn't arrived yet, but the old one has some new interventions. Michael Landy was not the only one to put his possessions on the line, or on the market. People have sold their lives (cars, houses, jobs) on the Internet, to recover from broken relationships or to rescue them from debt. Movements like Freeganism and Freebay seek to dodge the need for new things (even food), by giving new life to things rejected by others. Maybe a slow revolution is beginning?

But we mustn't hold our breath. New things are very easy to get hold of, despite the fact that we British don't seem to make many of them any more. In fact, the collapse of our old, physical industries into virtual industries is one of the oft-repeated signs of our troubled times. This has come at a huge and well-documented cost to individual lives, social cohesion, community identity. But does it have a cultural impact too?

Walk around the edgelands of Wolverhampton and you see a landscape struggling to shape itself to a world of virtual industry. The canal, once entirely functional, as a means of shifting goods and raw materials in and out, is now a place to walk or cycle in your lunch break. Most of what you see here is rubbish, or the business of rubbish. The old towpath itself is clean and green, but these edgelands businesses are recycling, or waste management, or breaker's yards. They are hard-hat zones. Mountains of plastics, cardboard, metals are tended by refuse trucks and JCBs. And there's so much rubbish that it gets stuck in the teeth of the diggers, in the gaps between the hub caps and tyres of the trucks, empty Coke and Fanta bottles wedged tight, left in place, because if it wasn't them it would be other bottles, and it's a waste of time to prise them out each night.

*

Self-storage is big business these days. Operating out of purpose-built big sheds, boxy low-rise units on industrial estates, or the shells of former factories and depots, self-storage warehouses are like hotels for *things*, places where people unload their belongings from the backs of cars, stack them on to trolleys and push them into the sterile light and down the aisles to their allotted room. The opposite of going shopping.

Self-storage warehouses are our new lofts and sheds and airing cupboards and cellars and garages. Those spaces are either already full, or have been converted, tanked out, reinvented. Or, in our largest cities, we are living in them. De-cluttering is endemic, fuelled by property programmes and the minimalist interior-design features that shine from the pages of weekend newspapers and magazines. Even writers joined in, allowing their tidy desks, decorated with the artworks of friends and mineral mementoes foraged from the wild edges of the world, to be photographed. We want to be able to move around fluently, to go abroad to live and work for a while, to hedge our bets on our relationships and domestic arrangements; to down-size when the markets slump, or when we're older.

And so the low-rent edgelands themselves are good places for storage to take root. We can continue to hoard, and never get around to clearing our possessions out for good. CCTV and fences and 24-hour security means our things are safe, out in the edgelands, and we can sleep soundly. We know we can't take it with us, but by setting up a simple monthly direct debit we can shore up our identities, and never have to say goodbye in this lifetime.

*

Self-storage facilities might make good places for shrines. By reversing the tendency, we could allow our messy lives to proliferate and find instead – in these blank grey rooms with caged ceilings – a place for prayer, or at least silence, thought and contemplative study. A unit would need only a candle, or a reading lamp; a comfortable chair or cushion; perhaps one of those futons so popular a decade or two ago. We could drive a couple of miles and leave our lives behind us, park up, and lock ourselves in to relax and think uncluttered thoughts in our clean and peaceful rented space. One major drawback, though, is that self-storage depots can be quietly creepy. Every woman we spoke to told us how they liked to get in and out as quickly and expeditiously as possible. These are not places to hang around. Our shrine idea died a little every time a door boomed shut somewhere.

*

All through the Noughties we heard the stories: people were operating their business out of self-storage units; people were running martial-arts gyms or dance classes inside them; young bands were practising and recording demos in them, once the province of the garage; people were buying stuff and having it delivered to self-storage units, which they might then sell on, having never laid a finger on it; people were convicted of murder, having hidden bodies in them, once the province of cellars or crawl spaces or papered-over cupboards; people were hiding the materials for making bombs in them; people were using them as recycling depots, places to store and pick over the things that people actually did manage to throw away; people were spending whole days within their thousands of square feet.

Landfill

A man is spotted at a tip. He has taken a small jute sack from the boot of his car and pauses to check whether anyone is looking, before producing a two-pound claw hammer, which he proceeds to strike the sack with, very purposefully, breaking up whatever is inside. Eventually, his face flushed, and satisfied, he throws it into the compressor. You wonder what the bag might have contained: a human jawbone, set with incriminating molars and dental work? A set of slate-blue, cobalt alloy hard drives?

In Joseph D'Lacey's *Garbage Man*, Stig is the name of a gate-keeper guarding a huge landfill near the fictional town of Shreve, somewhere in the English Midlands. Stig has grown accustomed to the lights of lorries approaching the perimeter fence in the dead of night, and to the handfuls of dirty twenties passed from the cab to buy his silence. He turns a blind eye to a county's unauthorised waste, its overrun quotas and the backlogs created by broken hospital incinerators; he turns a blind eye to the unauthorised waste of *other* counties, the noxious and borderline hazardous material driven for miles down motorways, then A-roads, then feeder lanes on to the site. People are always going to want to bury things out of mind, he reasons: there will always be waste, and its attendant managers and engineers, and the way things are going Stig has amassed a small fortune. The Stig of fifty years ago, guardian of a portal to the Neolithic and childhood adventures, has grown up into a very different Stig, one who now takes backhanders and has *scaled up*.

★

Rubbish is part of the texture of edgelands. It can be encountered singly here, often in surreal juxtaposition: a fly-tipped sofa in a corner of a turnip field; an electric cooker rusting under a bridge arch; a mattress anywhere open to the elements. We see things on their journey through from one category to another, often losing their identities in the process, as in Sean O'Brien's poem 'After Lafourge':

> – ambitious settees in black frogskin

> And minibars missing their castors, the catalogues
> Turning to mush, the unnameable objects
> That used to be something with knobs on,
> And now they live here, by the siding, the fishhouse,
> The building whose function is no longer known.

So much of what we find in the edgelands feels contingent. Outside of both urban centres and national parkland, regulatory frameworks tend to slacken and all forms of surveillance and policing are patchier. It's easier to build things there, but also to throw them away, to bury them. There are big fines to discourage those who try to avoid paying disposal taxes, but nobody's looking.

★

The edgelands become a place of forgetting, never more so than when they are used for dumping or for landfill, a place to put things out of mind on an industrial scale. 'The mind is not a landscape,' the poet Richard Wilbur once wrote, though if it were, that nagging, uncomfortable place we call the back of our minds might look like a landfill site. We all feel as if space might be finally running out in our lifetimes, or certainly our children's lifetimes: a background hum of unfocused but all-pervading guilt and anxiety. The adjective toxic is enjoying a new currency, its lexical value increasing as share prices fall towards the end of the Noughties, fastening itself to our property, debt, even upbringings: some of us had toxic childhoods. Beneath all of our worldly dealings, all our getting and spending, run deep, unspoken channels, drumlins of guilt.

*

Live landfill sites are an assault on the senses. Even from a distance, you can hear the two-tone klaxons, the constant roar of diesel engines straining up a system of slopes, and the gulls, panicky and urgent. Then there is the smell: if you've been stuck behind a bin wagon in traffic on a hot day, then you have experienced its harsh contours, though nothing prepares you for the cloying, relentless reek of household waste up close. You wonder if landfill workers tend to suffer from anosmia (somebody should familiarise this by giving it a handier name: 'binman's nose'?), an inability to register smells; or if their olfactory bulbs have simply become desensitised over time.

Things change once the final layers of aggregate and soil have been laid down, the surfaces capped and dressed, and the landscapers have tried their best, like undertakers, to restore some semblance of respectability. On the banks of the Lune just west of Lancaster (covering an area you could easily fit the city centre in to) lies Salt Ayre. A vast low mound, grassed over and dotted here and there with gorse: horses graze on it, cars pass by it, and an air of calm hangs over it. Salt Ayre has come to the end of its working life as a landfill site now, but get up close and it still feels very much alive. Beneath our feet lie over fifty years' worth of decomposing material, unknowable subterranean shiftings and settlings, slow collapses and fermentations. Grease and bone, paper and wood, glass, metals, solvents, rubber, dyes, fly ash, fat-trap waste . . .

Salt Ayre cross-sectioned, cut like a pie to reveal the strata of waste, or a deep core sample drawn from the ground. Here we can clearly see the fine veins of Christmas tree needles marking Januaries, a definite band that marks the UK Electricity Act and the first Non-Fossil Fuel Obligation orders, the gradual innundation of plastics and particleboard as we rise through the layers of years. Deep down, at the lowest levels, lie the peelings and scrapings of teatimes when Clement Attlee was Prime Minister. Vast colonies of microorganisms are busy at work in the dark. Leachate oozes from the ground into collection runnels and pipes, the compressed juice of the decades. Do we just imagine it, or does the ground give off heat?

Landfill sites are one of the few places you can still see the will-o'-the-wisp, or marsh lights, in twenty-first-century England. Methane burns with a pale bluish, flickering flame best seen at night, but people who live near landfill sites will be used to seeing it in flares. This is English folklore on steroids, a ghost running on industrial megawatts. Even as recently as the Eighties, pipes were pushed deep into the landfill and their vents lit with a burning, oily rag. Nowadays, methane is tapped off to generate power. Uncontrollable leaks of gas have been seen catching light spontaneously, flickering into ripples of life for a moment; then all is dark again. Lateral drift and build-up of this gas has been linked to all kinds of health problems in humans; an important part of waste management is tracking and controlling methane.

Picture the scene: the City Council Chambers in the damp autumn of 1950. A blue haze of cigarette and pipe smoke. A joint proposal has been put forward by Lancaster City Council and Morecambe and Heysham Town Council to establish a controlled tip (nobody uses the word 'landfill' yet) on Salt Ayre Marsh. The Corporation has already bought 185 acres of marshland, and proposes to raise its level nine inches by tipping. It's calculated to provide space for the next seventeen years, with further enclosure bringing more land into use step by step. But a reference back has been made: Councillor Mrs Pickard is worried about the effects of such a tip on house prices. Grit, dirt and a noxious smell would most likely carry westwards towards built-up areas and the city itself (a hangover from what academics would call 'the long nineteenth century': most industrialised areas tended to site their poorer dwellings to the east of a city, where the prevailing winds would carry airborne particulate, smoke and smells). Councillor T. S. Hayton seconds Councillor Pickard's reservations: it would be asking for trouble. But, as Alderman Simpson explains, these points have already been considered by the Committee. The Town Clerk points out that they will find the word 'controlled' mentioned in regard of tipping, so there is no question of nuisance. Only four members vote in favour of the amendment, the proposal is carried, and so a great space for forgetting called Salt Ayre is born.

*

Salt Ayre also became an unplanned ecosystem. Gulls, being great generalists, managed to establish a huge colony, the landfill providing a reliable source of edible (if putrescent) scraps, although studies have suggested that the birds might also be attracted to the relative scarcity of human activity, and the opportunity for mass social interaction. From the opposite bank of the Lune, Salt Ayre seethed with gulls from dawn till dusk. Humans came, too: gypsies, dwellers of margins and edges. By the early Seventies a camp had been established just adjacent to the site, though later that decade the local press were reporting a 'reign of terror' as the Council attempted to clamp down on 'illegal scavenging'. We have little record – these are secret, unwritten histories – of how it was or is for gypsies living with waste and scrap, and have to imagine the way in which their relationship to the world and its things are so materially different from our own. We might gain some sense of it from artists like Jimmie Durham, a Cherokee who grew up in Arkansas in the Forties and Fifties:

I expect it is no longer true, but when I was young towns still had edges, no-man's-lands, that were not yet the surrounding farms. This was where the city's refuse was casually dumped, so that the edge of town was not a 'natural' place. There lived raccoons, opossums, rats, snakes, bobcats, skunks, hobos who were in fact outlaws (not homeless street people), families of African Americans and displaced Indians. All of us, shunned by the city, used the city's surplus. I so loved the dumps, where one could find the products of civilization elegantly, surrealistically juxtaposed with pieces of wood, magic rocks, bones, and wild flowers, that they have remained the metaphor by which I define myself.

Salt Ayre could swallow anything. In November 2000 the corpse of a forty-foot female fin whale, stranded in Morecambe Bay, was carried by flatbed truck to Salt Ayre, where it was buried using a crane.

*

Jimmie Durham is not alone in his admiration of those skunks, raccoons and hobos living off his city's edgelands rubbish. Their resourcefulness, resilience and unshakeable drive to provide for their offspring have won them a reputation as welcome nocturnal visitors, rather than dirty bin-raiders.

In one of the American poet Robert Lowell's most celebrated poems 'Skunk Hour' – he describes a drive out at night to climb 'the hill's skull' in an attempt to find a way through a difficult time. 'My mind's not right,' he says in the poem:

> I hear
> my ill-spirit sob in each blood cell,
> as if my hand were at its throat . . .
> I myself am hell.

Lowell later said of the poem, 'This is the dark night. I hope my readers would remember John of the Cross' poem. My night is not gracious, but secular, puritan, agnostic.' Then, at this lowest ebb, close to despair, he sees the scavengers, a skunk family out on the prowl for food scraps, and the animals become an image of defiance, steadfastness, the will to survive, the mother trying to find food for her young in our garbage:

> She jabs her wedge head in a cup
> of sour cream, drops her ostrich tail,
> and will not scare.

*

'When the seagulls follow the trawler, it is because they think sardines will be thrown into the sea.' These words, by the footballer, film star and amateur philosopher Eric Cantona, might have been a baffling way to close a press conference after his infamous kung fu attack on a Crystal Palace fan, but they do contain an essential truth. Gulls, like rats, have learned that human behaviour is sufficiently profligate and chaotic that food will likely turn up if you follow the humans.

This has led – to the horror of many local authorities – to large and sometimes aggressive herring gulls flocking farther and farther inland, to settle on our landfill sites, bin-bag-strewn back alleys and city centre car parks. If you start to look for them, you see more and more. It looks like a slow, Hitchcockian takeover. Their noise, their rapid rate of breeding and the noxious and copious white streaks they leave across cars, buildings, pavements, have caused many councils, and indeed the Scottish Parliament, to see them as a significant problem. But the herring gull's story is far from straightforward. While the inland gulls of our disused factories and landfill sites are establishing successful and fast-growing colonies, the old coastal colonies are on the wane. The situation is so severe now that the RSPB has put herring gulls on their 'red' list of endangered species. So while councils seek to control and lessen the impact of these large, intrusive birds, they must also seek to protect them. Clearly, if you are a gull, the allure of a windy cliff cannot match that of a massive, fetid landfill site. Perhaps we are witnessing the shift of a bird population from coastal to edgelands and urban? Then the name 'herring gull', like that of the 'pointer' or 'Portuguese Water Dog', will become a device for remembering the past, a source of curiosity for our children's children: 'They lived near the sea then? And what's a herring?'

*

John Clare knew the will-o'-the-wisp: 'Will with a whisp, Jack Whisk, Jack with a lanthorn.' His village, Helpston, to the west of Peterborough lay close to the meres and fenland that clung on, still partially undrained and intact, into the beginning of the nineteenth century, and he had seen strange lights, as he describes here with typical accuracy and precision in his journal:

> – I have seen several there myself one night when returning home from Ashton on a courting excursion I saw one as if meeting me I felt very terrified & on getting to a stile I determnd to wait & see if it was a person with a lanthorn or a will o whisp it came on steadily as if on the path way & when it got near me within a poles reach perhaps as I thought it made a sudden stop as if to listen me I then believed it was some one but it blazd out like a whisp of straw & made a crackling noise like straw burning which soon convinced me of its visit the luminous haloo that spread from it was of a mysterious terrific hue & the enlargd size & whiteness of my own hands frit me the rushes appeard to have grown up as large & tall as whalebone whips & the bushes seemd to be climbing the sky every thing was extorted out of its own figure & magnified the darkness all round seemd to form a circalar black wall & I fancied that if I took a step forward I shoud fall into a bottomless gulph which seemed yawning all round me . . .

Clare's Swordy Well became a landfill site for a time. Swordy Well was an area of limestone grazing land that had established itself around the remnants of an old quarry, and for Clare it was a place of work (looking after livestock), but also idle play, indolence or 'botanizing'. Clare is the pre-eminent poet of noticing things in the world, of our need to connect with and properly inhabit the places where we live and work:

> I've loved thee, Swordy Well, and love thee still:
> Long was I with thee, tending sheep and cow
> In boyhood, ramping up each steepy hill
> To play at 'roly poly' down – and now
> A man I trifle o'er thee cares to kill,
> Haunting thy mossy steeps to botanize
> And hunt the orchis tribes where nature's skill
> Doth like my thoughts run into fantasies–
> Spider and bee all mimicking at will,
> Displaying powers that fools the proudly wise,
> Showing the wonders of great nature's plan
> In trifles insignificant and small,
> Puzzling the power of that great trifle man,
> Who finds no reason to be proud at all.

Swordy Well was common land, but Clare grew up to see his landscape disintegrate and his connections to it severed as enclosure changed ancient boundaries and landmarks, diverted watercourses, grubbed up old trees and hedges; in seeing this he also registered what happens when land is disposed as property, as something with monetary value above all else.

Swordy Well has been many things since Clare's time. Ravers used it as a site for parties. It used to be a racetrack for stock-car meets. Swaddywell Pit (as it is now known) lies behind a modern stone yard, down a path that leads from the main road. There's an interpretation board at the gate, a sure sign that things have changed: Swaddywell is now a nature reserve. But as recently as the Eighties it was used as a dump. Local people remember lorries and lights on the tip late in the night and, even now, in some of the lower reaches of the footpath that loops around the site, the ground is iridescent with slimy discharges oozing from the earth. Nobody can tell us exactly what was dumped here. Amazingly, though, Clare's orchids are still evident, and in abundance: the meadowland where the tip was capped is carpeted today in bee and pyramidal varieties. There is wild carrot and yellow wort. Grasshopper warblers reel in the sedge and undergrowth; common darter, four-spotted chaser, emperor and black-tailed skimmer dragonflies cruise the air.

*

Experts have managed to identify the location of a painting by John Constable, a near contemporary of Clare's, that lies fifty miles or so eastwards in Suffolk. *The Stour Valley and Dedham Village* of 1815 has been carefully compared to the present landscape, and the artist's view finally found. In his day, Constable fretted over whether landscape painting could ever be regarded as art, writing about 'a sad freak with which I have long been "possessed" of feeling a duty – on my part – to tell the world that there is such a thing as Landscape existing with "Art" – as I have in so great measure failed to "show" the world that it is possible to accomplish it'.

What strikes us immediately, flipping between a reproduction of the original painting and a photograph of the view today taken to scale, is the physical difference in the earth, the lie of the land. Perhaps it's only natural to try and imagine some pristine viewpoint, some correlation with what an artist looked at centuries before. In their own ways, both Constable and Clare were precise, and devoted to place. Standing in the meadowland at Swordy Well, the imagination begins its work, Photoshopping out the modern pylons and telegraph poles, altering the growth of trees in a kind of reverse time lapse, looking for older landmarks. What we should realise, though, is that over time the land itself is in flux. Earth is moved about, shifted, disturbed. There are excavations, ploughings, all manner of mineral extraction, backfilling, infilling, blasting. We want to fix and identify some enduring and underlying aspect, as if there is, in the past, some timeless, ideal condition that lies waiting to be uncovered.

What there is, here at Swaddywell, is a new ecosystem, flourishing on a chance alignment of drainage and a particular mix of different soils and substrate; naturally occurring geology mixed with materials – rubbish – brought from elsewhere. Insects and birds and wildflowers are not interested in aesthetics. All that matters is a biological opportunity. The earth is in motion, simply a much slower version of the cloud studies Constable made when he turned his attention to the English skies.

*

There have been artists for whom rubbish in the landscape is treated as primary matter and subject. Keith Arnatt had become an established conceptual artist by the beginning of the Seventies, but moved away from his avant-garde origins (and lost the patronage of the art establishment in the process: the major galleries that had once supported him stopped showing and collecting his work) to concentrate on black-and-white photography. His work became difficult to classify. He was drawn to landscape, and in each series of work such as *Abandoned Landscapes*, *A.O.N.B* and *The Forest*, he suggests a new kind of English sublime. He began to explore what he called 'the conjunction of "beauty" and "banality"'. An oil drum rusts on its side in front of an old stone wall; sheets of battered corrugated iron stand against a scrubby brake of trees (topped by an implausible, ad hoc sign for BOILER FUEL); cords of timber, spray-painted by a woodcutter, lie incongruously against a misty forest backdrop; ash spoil from a fly-tip fire cools on the bank of a misty lake; a silvery current of time and human absence seems to flow through them all.

Perhaps it was only a matter of time before Arnatt found himself photographing landfill. He moved into colour, making images along a track in the Forest of Dean for a series called *Miss Grace's Lane* (1986–7): human detritus and nature form compositions full of echoes of Samuel Palmer, the landscape artist working out of his 'Rat Abbey' cottage near Shoreham a century and a half earlier: Arnatt referred to the images he made here as his 'polythene Palmers'. Bin bags burst, disgorging their contents on to the raw dolomite and sandstone earth; a red carrier bag snarled in a stand of bulrushes glows; a lorry tyre broods in a dark shallow pool at the end of a path; upturned car wrecks and abandoned giant soft toys vie for maximum incongruity in the long grass; a brilliant plastic green watering can stands next to the rosebay that didn't need its help.

This is the work of an artist noticing things in the landscape without recourse to judgement or polemic, but for his next photographs Arnatt tightened the focus upon objects discovered at Colford Tip and Howler's Hill landfill site near his home. In doing so, his work moved away from landscape and closer to still life, in art historical terms a genre of lower ranking, somehow regarded as less important. Our sense of scale is broken down as we study our discarded matter, caught in the act of falling apart. What we now see is the world of things after the careful husbandry and season-defying displays of the supermarket shelf, and Arnatt's insistence and attention has been reserved for these hidden or neglected afterlives. These works are as studied and composed as traditional still lifes, organic putrefaction and the durability of plastics shot in the magic hour, the warm, angled light of evening. Eggshells, rinds, spaghetti, sponge cake, all are captured in extremis, in their last moments as identifiable objects in this life. They are the work of a Chardin or Flegel for our age. Arnatt's work from this period forms one of the most beautiful, sustained and overlooked explorations into our edgelands.

*

Visiting our rivers, parks, golf courses, lakes and mountain tops, or the heritage sites where famous writers and artists once lived, in the past few years people have increasingly happened upon spoors of human ash. By the end of the Noughties, so many people were scattering the ashes of loved ones at beauty spots that the Environment Agency had to issue a leaflet. Football clubs had to halt the goalmouth and corner-flag sacraments. Perhaps the ultimate test of how we regard our waste is the way we dispose of our dead, which is a form of landfill. As the academic Robert Pogue Harrison puts it, we should be grateful we live on a planet that provides us with somewhere to put our dead; for the hiding and receiving power of 'this terracqueous globe' we live on. The dead first have to disappear in order that their souls can attain an afterlife among the living.

Edgelands internments or scatterings are unacceptable. The idea immediately calls to mind criminal disposal and effacement, the dismembered parts of a body dispersed in a necropolis of motorway pillars and incinerators and car crushers as incriminating evidence. Bodies in landfill suggest the same, or worse, some kind of dystopian mass grave. The idea of a funeral service on a patch of wasteland or a mausoleum inside the railed-off gravel of an electricity substation shows just how unsettled and starkly utilitarian we regard these places. Unconsecrated ground. The soul would surely enter limbo.

It's become possible – indeed, desirable – to have an environmentally responsible funeral these days. There has been a significant movement towards new kinds of burial apparatus and sites, including woodland areas that by careful management will process the dead until the site becomes open and accessible to all within a few generations. But recycling the dead means we lose the spaces we consecrate and remember them by. Memorialising serves a social purpose. Still, the topsoil and substrate is on the move – it just takes time – and, this late in the day, it's difficult to imagine a place in the ground that doesn't contain some trace of us. We are everywhere, even in the air. Those beautiful sunsets in our western skies are caused by the sun's rays travelling obliquely through the atmosphere at its deepest, picking up, in among all the fly ash and pollen and particulate, our human dust.

Water

When Alfred Wainwright – walker and cartographer – died in 1991, his ashes were scattered on the shores of a pool in his beloved Lake District. Set among the fells known as 'Haystacks', this standing water was Wainwright's favourite spot, described by the author as

> a quiet place, a lonely place. I shall go to it, for the last time, and be carried: someone who knew me in life will take me and empty me out of a little box and leave me there alone. And if you, dear reader, should get a bit of grit in your boot as you are crossing Haystacks in the years to come, please treat it with respect. It might be me.

To add to the romance, this pool in question is known as 'Innominate Tarn'. Innominate, as in unnamed or unclassified. This, surely, is one of England's wild places, quiet and lonely, as Wainwright said, bleak and exposed, its wilderness quality evoked by the namelessness of its name.

But what if most of us lived within half an hour's drive of pools even lonelier and bleaker than a Lakeland tarn, unvisited, unseen, pools so unclassified that nobody thinks to give them names? Beyond 'innominate', these are pools that don't have names because they don't need them. Loved landscapes, lived-in landscapes, need a litany of names so we can map our stories across them. The Welsh-language poet Waldo Williams, writing fifty years ago in rural Wales, brought into his work not just the names of rivers, villages, woodlands and farms, but the names of individual fields. England's edgelands include not just fields but ash copses between broken factory walls, fathomless lakes, scrublands vivid with wild flowers, almost all unmapped and unseen. How 'unseen'? This is the paradox of edgelands. Feral as they are, a no-man's-land between the watched and documented territories of urban and rural, the edgelands are a passing place, backdrop for countless commuters, shoppers, rail travellers. Seen, but unseen. Looked at but not into.

When Roy Fisher published his groundbreaking long poem 'City' in 1961 he said of Birmingham (his home city, and the 'city' of the poem) 'most of it has never been seen'. Now our cities have been seen. And how. Cameras tilt like cathedral gargoyles from the roofs of every office or shop, not to ward off ill fortune, but to capture it in shaky monochrome. Our cities have been studied, mapped and celebrated as keenly as our countryside. The same cannot be said of our edgelands.

*

So many vehicles have, in film, found themselves careening into the depths of a gravel pit or flooded quarry that it would be entirely possible to edit together and assemble a short piece of avant-garde cinema from the available footage. When we look into the murk of standing water, we can imagine the imponded cars of the Fifties and Sixties and Seventies, weedy wrecks, and death traps all over again waiting for the unwary swimmer, the reckless divers who will come each year during spells of unseasonal heat. Deep standing water fascinates because of what it might contain, because of the riddle of depth and a corresponding, deep-seated idea of the bottomless. Even though we know this water isn't going anywhere, there is also a fantasy of watery connectedness, as if every pond and pit is somehow linked via subterranean conduits like cold and cloudy northern versions of the Yucatan sinkhole or *cenote*. The surfaces that give back only our leaden, flake-white skies seem to be hiding something, thoughts that lead us down, down.

*

Two ponds. The first is a childhood pond, and has the blank stare of Thomas Hardy's 'Neutral Tones', a study in greys and mid-tones that gives little away, all under a sky 'chidden of God'. We approach this pond from the housing estate, which in this case is called Naylorsfield, though it could be any one of those estates that peter out into backfields and farmland. In the middle distance is the M62, having just left Liverpool; you are aware of its soft roar long before you realise its source. Eventually, you come upon the pond; low clumps of hawthorn give it away before you see the water. Nobody knows why this pond is here and nobody knows its name. It is forsaken: a red plastic milk crate catches the eye, marooned in the grey reedy shallows; slowly, the shape of an abandoned car forms in the deeper water like a photograph in the developing tray. Beyond this, at its centre, the unknowable depths. Anglers used to fish here, catapulting meal riddled with thread-worms into their swims, but their peace had been too often disturbed by kids off the estate, who liked nothing better than detonating the depth charge of a half brick in the pond's centre, and now nobody comes.

The second pond is a recent unexpected joy. This is John Clare country, on the outskirts of Peterborough, the last of a limestone heath before the flat land of the Fens. The arable land has a businesslike feel here, refusing to be accepted into 'the countryside' proper; the path to the pond leaves the back road via a lay-by, which, judging by the amount of used condoms festooning the hedgerow and cigarette butts in the camber, is a well-used dogging spot. Pylons crackle overhead. The heathland is disturbing somehow, the authentic, unkempt English landscape that doesn't know what to do with itself. On the walk to the pond you soon tune into whitethroats and chiffchaffs in the scrub. Suddenly, it's there, on the edge of a wood, dark and inviting. The water is bottle green, and its margins are endlessly intriguing to the eye: this pond uses all the tricks of bulrushes and reeds, high bank then low shoreline, actually revealing a foot-wide slope of muddy beach the colour of unset mortar. It is a pond rich in detail, a Pre-Raphaelite vision with the focus now screwed tight and sharp, now scrimmed and soft, touched with the colours of wild flowers in the summer months.

In a way, both ponds are lenses: the former rheumy, opaque as a cataract, the latter a portal into the nineteenth century. All over England, ponds just like them have claimed the lives of children, on summer afternoons separated by decades.

*

Nobody can agree on a pond. Where exactly does a pool end and a pond begin? When does a pond become a lake? According to the charity Pond Conservation:

> A pond is a man-made or natural waterbody which is between 1m2 [sic] and 2 hectares (this is equivalent in size to about 2.5 football pitches), which holds water for four months of the year or more.

Other definitions take into account water clarity, and the portion of bottom reached by sunlight. But such attempts to define lead us away from the essential mystery of ponds, the way they inhere in time alongside us. Time is everything. Ponds develop out of the raw ingredients for life, each one a tiny parable of creation. The poets have plumbed their 'stilled legendary depth', as Ted Hughes describes it:

> A pond I fished, fifty yards across,
> Whose lilies and muscular tench
> Had outlasted every visible stone
> Of the monastery that planted them . . .

Man-made ponds can outlive their function. Surface workings left to flood can become symbols of neglect and forgetting, as the world moves on. Gravel is 'won' nearby its intended destination and use – it is the basest of minerals, and not worth transporting any great distance – so the flooded pits near our estates and rail yards and factories are in fact their negative spaces, remnants that might easily outlast them.

*

Now we know why familiarity breeds contempt. Studies into memory suggest that it tailors its work to suit the task. At life-changing moments it lays down a thick, multi-tracked record of the car crash, the first kiss, the birth. So thick is the track that time seems to slow down as it passes. By contrast, if you drive the same piece of road each day, past the same stretch of scrub and standing water, memory lays a track so thin it merely serves to keep your past, present and future in the right order. No need for detail, no home cinema required.

Nine miles south of Manchester, where two roads cross, two nameless strips of water mirror the (usually grey) skies. Here, fast traffic to Britain's second busiest airport crosses a commuter artery on a short flyover. Tucked between the airport hangar architecture of a health and fitness club and a clump of self-seeded trees lies a kidney-shaped pool. Sometimes, at weekends, a car or two is parked at the side of the health club's slip road and fishermen spend a few hours sitting at the side of this innominate pool.

Can there be fish in it? Local word suggests there must be, because the fishermen keep coming back. But how did the fish get there, in a pool without a history, without a maker? No glacier formed this, no river feeds it. Maybe these edgelands fish self-seeded here, evolved from insects in the dry soil, nameless themselves and featureless as cave fish. In the markets and fishmongers of Manchester they lie between the silver and steel of salmon, trout, shark, as blank as ice, unnoticed. How would they taste, these innominate fish? Well, if this pool is the opposite of sea – a half-day's drive to any coast, fed by rain and water table, orphaned water – then think of it as sweet not salt, and the fish flesh as muscovado caramel.

*

If sea-fish stocks continue to collapse, it isn't entirely fanciful to imagine wet counters that deal entirely in catch from the standing water belting the outlying fields and waste ground of our most spartan estates. Instead of the silvers and gunmetals and blooms of pink we associate with sea fish, these would present an altogether different still-life palette: the loose-change colours of roach, minnows, rudd; the dun greys and mud tones and bronzings of big tench, fresh in their cauls of slime; a shoal display of perch, spiny and waspish, arranged in multitudinous dartings that mirror the starlings of the air above; and pike, the centrepiece, the familiar torpedo shape and prehistoric jaw. The fishmonger might indulge a flair for drama by inserting a smaller fish, head first, into the maw of an especially large specimen. The whole display might oftentimes be garnished with the tangled pondweed and milfoils found in the gravel pits that supplied each catch.

*

But nobody comes and, left to itself, unmanaged, standing water quietly offers its opportunities to the wildlife edged out of our countryside by the homogenising, flattening effects of agribusiness, a last refuge for those unlovable creatures that once dwelt in fens and meres and troughs, a place where things might start all over again.

Even the medicinal leech clings on in a few muddy pools and ditches. Once prized for its use in controlled exsanguinations meant to balance the bodily humours, it suffered centuries of over-exploitation and is only found now very locally, including a handful of Sites of Special Scientific Interest. You can feel the decline by the beginning of the nineteenth century in Wordsworth's poem 'Resolution and Independence', where the old leech-gatherer who roams from pond to pond tells us:

'Once I could meet with them on every side;
But they have dwindled long by slow decay;
Yet still I persevere, and find them where I may.'

In a way though, the leech lives on as a distillation of what we might fear beneath the surface of all standing water. It's as if our distaste for pools and ponds issues from some primitive, mammalian, creaturely concern for the far older world they contain.

Unswept by cleansing currents, the nastiness seems to concentrate, a sump of hydras and worms; their alien, parasitic life cycles banishing them from Nature, and our sense of the pastoral. Still, our ancestor's bloodletting reliance on the leech has admitted it on to the protected species lists as its range in this country has guttered down like a draining inland sea.

*

Just across the road from the fishing pool, a seasonal wetland flourishes. Lost between a household storage depot stuffed with overspill chattels and a freight yard delivering new chattels in gleaming vans, this is not a place to walk. It can be glimpsed by car, if you know where to look. But it's easy to miss. This is not a sprawling marsh. Edgelands landscapes grow in gaps, changing as they cross a road, circle a building. This is outer Manchester. If people want city they drive into it. If they want country they head east to the Peaks or north to the Lakes. No one looks at this.

But for a brief period this roadside fen was noticed. In a last-ditch attempt to eke out some value from the land, its owner fenced it off and made it home for a family of water buffalo. The story made the regional TV news, and for a while cars would slow and children point at the dark beasts up to their hooftops in Manchester rain. In the summer, the land dried out and the buffalo were gone. Red-brown spears of sorrel burst from the soil as if their seeds had been rusted in the winter soak, and purple thistles formed their own fences within fences, fields within a nameless field. The fields in Waldo Williams' Welsh poems carry names like 'Weun Parc Y Blawd' – 'Flower Meadow Field' – but what name might this seasonal marsh field carry? Buffalo Fen Field? Rust Thistle Meadow?

In the dry summer, when the buffalo have shrivelled back into the soil like giant lungfish, makeshift advertising boards stand where they once stood, calling the attention of drivers seeking diet plans, cheap laptops and get-rich-quick schemes. But the buffalo are waiting, buried and ready for the monsoon to slake and wake them.

*

To invert Heraclitus: any man might step into the same pond twice. Might there still be ponds – behind factory walls, on the far side of nettle-carpeted tips, invisible from the main road – where time has thickened, an imperceptible convection of algae and slimes, where sunlight itself seems to slow to a final few persistent photons among the single-celled denizens of the pond bed? If the fast-flowing stream or river is possessed of current, then ponds and gravel pits might be said to be cells themselves, self-possessed, simple batteries converting sunlight into energy. Though any child taken pond-dipping knows how complex standing water can feel, how any trawl with a simple bamboo net yields up intricate water beetles and boatmen. It's like taking an old watch apart, its pieces spinning and winding down on the bankside. Perhaps it's this intricacy, this concentratedness, which can quicken our attention. In the same way a rocket frozen in mid-flight is said to *contain* its velocity, so mature standing water is teeming with contained possibility.

*

Standing water was the edgeland of our ancestors. The ancient Celts looked at the surface of pools and lakes and saw a shifting screen that separated their world from the world of their gods.

Welsh and Irish museums are full of votive offerings found in standing water – torques and bracelets, brooches and goblets – cast into the water to assuage the anger of the gods. Whatever was of value, worthy of honour, was fair game for a drowning. A few years ago, a young curator in the National Museum in Dublin would confess to you – if asked – that the well-preserved barrels of so-called 'bog butter' dumped by prehistoric tribes in their local marshes tasted 'a bit like cream cheese, and quite nice actually'. 'You ate some?' 'Just a sliver, on a cracker. I couldn't resist it.'

Nine miles south of 'Buffalo Fen Field' in a marsh called Lindow Moss, builders in the Eighties found a body and the police were called. Detailed study and carbon dating confirmed that the body did indeed appear to be a murder victim, but the murder took place two thousand years ago. Since known as 'Lindow Man', this twisted leather corpse now sprawls in a glass case under museum lights. This was not the afterlife he'd hoped for as, acting out his priestly duty for his tribe, he was painted green with vegetable dye, garrotted with a cord and cast into the marshy water as a sacrificial victim. Now, we still cast the symbols of what we value into water. Edgelands pools are cluttered with shopping trolleys, car tyres, beer cans. Imagine the illicit thrill of a young curator in a future 'Museum of Blair's England', taking one heady sip from a bottle of flat 'fen cola', then screwing the cap on and sticking it back in the glass case.

Sewage

Coming upon a sewage farm in the landscape, we're as far as it's possible to be from deep, old England, the England of rills and rain on oak leaves. If clear water has flown through the English imagination – from the late medieval hymn to the Virgin: 'Haill fresche fontane that springis new, the rute and crope of all virtù . . .' all the way to Philip Larkin's 'devout drench' – then this is its dark, divergent stream, a Stygian sludge to be dealt with in the edgelands.

Although nobody calls them 'sewage farms' any more. Or even 'sewage works'. There are several ways of treating raw sewage today, though a hundred years ago the practice really did resemble farming: either tracts of land were irrigated with waste or it was collected in shallow lagoons on porous soil, in order to allow biological oxidation to take place; this land was rotated, ploughed and allowed to return to cultivation once dried. Paradoxically, the prudish Victorians happily and routinely referred to the 'filth' they were dealing with where raw sewage was concerned, even in august organs such as the *British Medical Journal*. Try to imagine 'filth management centres' – and realise how the terms for dealing with our human waste effluent have been in flight from their modern, nineteenth-century origins. Nowadays, 'greywater' and 'blackwater' are separated en route to a 'water treatment plant'. Language itself has been sanitised.

*

In September 2008 Yorkshire Water invited its customers to take part in a simple quiz. The prize: a behind-the-scenes tour of its Esholt sewage works, near Bradford, where the equivalent of 112 Olympic-sized swimming pools of waste gets treated every day. One of the questions concerned the tomato plant ('Name one of the most unlikely places you'll see tomato plants sprouting?'). As these kinds of questions often are, it seemed deliberately easy, for, as everybody knows, tomato seeds survive their transit through the human gut and can germinate in skips full of sludge and toilet paper, even surviving further in the medium of farmland compost, to sprout roguishly among crops.

Sewage farms always suggest the scale of our settlements, collective bodily functions and a kind of community. All of us – bar the isolated devotees of the septic tank, or the commune's earthen-pit users – are distantly connected and plumbed in to these lagoons and basins. Children adventurous enough to approach their meshing and gaze into their simple geometric playgrounds grasp the interdependencies and size of a city or region by means of a simple scatological arithmetic, and, like power stations, they generate their own myths of profligacy and danger. They are one of the easiest man-made constructions to identify from Google Earth, once you've got your eye in: set into the hinterlands of every sizeable town or conurbation, their percolating filters lie like dark dials. These are the preferred vehicles for oxidising our sewage today, grim merry-go-rounds filled with clinker, slag or gravel. Children have even been known to ride them, and what could be more fun than running across a crust as thin as cat ice formed on the surface of a sludge lagoon?

*

Perhaps sewage farms will become obsolete, if we all take up the call by some green campaigners to create tree bogs. These are eco-toilets built in woods or gardens, in which carefully chosen plants – willows and nettles are commonly cited – are used to surround and protect a kind of compost heap on stilts, with the sewage itself protected from rodents by layers of chicken wire and straw.

The object of the exercise is to turn human waste into biomass, literally feeding our sewage back into the ground to produce stronger growth in nutrient-hungry plants. These vigorous plants and trees can then be cut and used for many purposes. An edge-lands tree bog could feed willows, which could then be cut to build tree houses and dens. The tree bog – if properly constructed – need never be emptied, it simply deals with anything we drop in.

Imagine dog-walkers and joggers pausing at an edgelands tree bog to contribute a little something to the 'tree-house fund'.

*

Approached at ground level, all is absolute fenced-off functionality, and in this way sewage farms also seem to resemble landlocked tanker decks, or chemical refineries, grassed over. These are un-designed places, in an aesthetic sense: nobody has worried over their clean lines, or suffered anything like a *horror vacui*. Under-writing our very civility, and keeping our lives sanitary and free from all kinds of disease, they toil anonymously in the edgelands, never to be looked at, hidden away from business and residential areas, unvisited.

But birds come. Sewage farms are birdy places. As microhabi-tats that exist in many different shapes and sizes, they can host important, even unique, communities of species. The birds find relatively quiet places with cover, nesting potential and a steady supply of food in the form of worms, insects and mites. Places to feed, or rest, or breed.

At the end of summer, as the nights begin to draw in again towards autumn, many people living in urban areas might think back fondly to trips they made into the Brecon Beacons, Dartmoor, the Lake District, the Yorkshire Dales. They remember that red kite in Wales, or the golden eagle that was probably only a buzzard soaring above the fells near Derwent Water. Our wildlife seems to be framed and sealed within the sunny day, the picturesque view, the tranquillity and silence of big open spaces.

But so far as birds are concerned, early autumn is the beginning of rush hour, and it's passing by so much closer to where most of us actually live, through the edgelands. Migrant passerines are gearing up, collecting in small sewage works: yellow wagtails, redstarts, spotted flycatchers, and many species of warbler, gathering to feed on the last hatches of insects, the first berry fruits. Pipits and wagtails are forming small flocks on larger irrigation plots and lagoons. Shorebirds and waders are on the move: sandpiper, redshank, green-shank, dunlin, ruff and snipe, are all commonly found in different party mixtures and combinations. Then there are the rarities.

Pallas's, Radde's and dusky warblers, the trumpeter finch, pectoral and marsh sandpipers, the long-billed dowitcher, the north American green-winged teal . . . Birds that breed or winter in Siberia and Asia and the Americas and Africa, all have been found inter-mittently in the sewage works and lagoons and sludge pools under leaden English skies, within a mile or two of major roads and busi-ness parks. The wilderness with good links to the coast.

*

Birds are able to seek out – have to seek out – the habitat conducive to their survival that lies in our midst. There's a strange ecological tautology here, in the way edgelands places, like sewage farms, have become so biodiverse as a by-product of dealing with our own human by-products. After a day spent traipsing along the muddy margins of the pools at Avonmouth sewage works, and being rewarded with good views of a snipe, we also wondered at the strange way our human, managed landscapes have provided a last refuge for certain species that would once have flourished. That snipe is making the most of a kind of landscape that would have once covered huge swathes of England, the fens to the east that once made up much of Cambridgeshire, Lincolnshire, Norfolk and Suffolk, and thousands of acres of undrained marshland everywhere else. Wisps of snipe would have once been a much commoner sight, and the bird was brought to table for hundreds of years: in his *Poly-Olbion* of 1622, the poet Michael Drayton, cataloguing the multitudinous birds of the fenlands, describes to us 'the pallat-pleasing *Snite*'. We wonder how snipe taken from a sewage farm would taste.

Two centuries later, in John Clare's poem 'To the Snipe', we recognise the 'lover of swamps' that now haunts sewage farms, finding its environment in our own, persisting in the overlooked edges:

> Boys thread the woods
> To their remotest shades,
> But in these marshy flats, these stagnant floods,
> Security pervades
>
> From year to year,
> Places untrodden lie

Where man nor boy nor stock hath ventured near
– Nought gazed on but the sky

And where there are birds, there are bound to follow birders. Or twitchers. Or birdwatchers. Or ornithologists. We have stumbled into a world threaded with tribal shibboleths and codes all of its own, even as soon as we try to give its people a name. According to Mark Cocker – who, in his book *Birders*, takes an almost ethnographic approach to this tribe he belongs to – 'birdwatcher' is simply too formal, passive and voyeuristic, and no self-respecting member of the bird tribe would use it (and woe betide the inserters of hyphens who would have us use 'bird-watcher'; while 'bird watcher' as two separate words requires some form of legal action). At the same time, the work of the 'ornithologist' has drifted, sadly, into the unforgiving dialects of the academy and beyond earshot of the bird tribe's legions of amateurs.

Which leaves 'birder' and 'twitcher'. The former is the more active designation of choice: not universally accepted, but your safest bet. 'Twitcher' is more often, especially in the mouths of other tribes, pejorative. Cocker traces its entry into the language back to the late Fifties, and attributes it to a small circle of birders working with Howard Medhurst, then a member of one of the earliest rarities committees. Turning up to verify sightings having ridden pillion on a motorbike in all weathers, people soon got used to Howard's shaking – a product of excitement, but also the onset of hypothermia – and 'being on a twitch' stuck. It chimes in an odd way with the English biker culture of the time, black-and-white footage of Johnny Kidd & the Pirates, whose biggest hit 'Shakin' All Over' came from a favourite phrase of their lead singer's, who liked to tell his mates how a pretty girl he'd seen in the street had sent excitable 'quivers down the membranes'.

A few twitchers have probably given the whole tribe a bad name. Anybody who has encountered the overzealous rarities-chaser accidentally in the field, and been made to feel as if they've blundered on to their very own private property, will sympathise with the view that twitchers are sad, tick-list obsessive, proprietorial goons who think nothing of travelling from one end of the country to the other having been paged about an unconfirmed sighting of a lanceolated warbler. But there is considerable overlap between 'twitcher' and 'birder'. Most birders would admit how they'd love to identify and report a species new to this country. In this way, any birder might find themselves engaged in a twitch, though the rarity might be local, and the business far less concerned with list envy or one-upmanship. Rarities themselves are, by definition, birds that have ended up for whatever reason in unusual or unexpected places.

Over the years, birders have got to know the edgelands better than most. Some sites and incidents have passed into legend: the ornithologist and birder Chris Mead falling into the sludge at Wisbech (and whose house, full of exhausted ringing volunteers, was raided by police hunting for the Great Train Robbers); Clive Byers, in search of the black-winged pratincole at Reading sewage works, being squirted with liquefied pigshit by an irate farmer, whose land he had crossed. Today, it would be unbecoming of any birder not to spend at least some time exploring sewage farms, as well as landfill sites and rubbish tips. Muddy in winter, stinking and flyblown in summer, but in many ways just as good as – and often better than – official reserves; although, ironically, finding a toilet can often be a problem.

*

Google Earth is turning out to be a useful tool for birders. A reconnaissance mission from a desk- or laptop can provide a bird's-eye view of the terrain, and sewage farms are easy to spot and assess; a practised eye can distinguish between the kinds of treatment and filtration being used, and gauge the level of foliage and cover. The armchair twitch is still a way off. Dropping towards the roofs and treetops on Google Earth offers nothing but a depopulated, lifeless England, frozen at some point in the very recent past. But this is changing, as the 'gallery' and 'street view' functions slowly try to collectively animate what's happening on the ground. The 'gallery' function in particular could contain 'twitch films' taken on-site. We swoop hopefully over Clare's village of Helpston, but only find a forty-one-second cameraphone film of teenagers hedge-jumping.

*

Rare birds, accidental visitors blown off their migratory courses or forced outside their ranges by weather, bring the global to our doorsteps. But while birders value these freak occurrences, our edgelands are shaped and influenced by huge global forces. Sewage-treatment plants are owned by private water companies, which in turn are owned – partly or wholly – by international private equity companies, pension funds and banks, as are many of our privatised utility companies, airports and so on. Imagine seeing a Lapland bunting at a sewage works just south of Peterborough. This isn't beyond the realms of possibility: the Lapland bunting isn't a huge twitch, though you do need to get east to stand a good chance of seeing them wintering in England. This part of the country's water supply is controlled and managed by Anglian (John Clare would have fallen into this catchment area), which is ultimately owned by, among other concerns, the Canadian Pension Plan Investment Board. This means you would be watching a bird that breeds in a range encompassing the circumpolar tundra, wintering on a facility owned by a Canadian company. You are probably using Austrian or German optics. Welcome to the global edgelands.

*

Just as the edgelands has its pastiche stone circles, planted on the roundabouts of business parks, so it has its pastiche ancient pathways. The Ridgeway is a 5,000-year-old track reputed to be the oldest road in England, tracing a chalk escarpment from Wiltshire to Buckinghamshire. But there is a new Ridgeway, an edgelands path riding the mound of London's 'Southern Outfall Sewer' at Plumstead. The new Ridgeway may not have the ancient landmarks of the old one – Uffington Castle, Avebury stone circle, Wayland's Smithy – but it does have an atmosphere all its own, offering the edgelands hiker a bird's-eye view of rooftops, gasometers and scrubland, all under the gaze of surveillance cameras. But the crowning glory of the new Ridgeway is the presence of Victorian London's favourite bird – the linnet. Once snared and blinded to encourage them to sing, these heathland birds are now protected, and clouds of linnets gather to feed in this green corridor. Their twittering chorus is the music of south London's edgelands. And if birdsong springs from sheer joy (one theory among many, but an appealing one) then these edgelands have their share of praise.

Not to be outdone by the 'Southern Outfall Sewer', the imaginatively titled 'Northern Outfall Sewer' has seen possibly the quintessential edgelands development. Here, in Stratford, east London, is a new viewing platform known as the 'View Tube', allowing visitors to witness the construction of the Olympic Park.

Why is it so exemplary? Well, the 'View Tube' is made out of stacked Freight Containers, is situated on top of a raised sewer, is making a recreational opportunity out of looking at a building site, and has built-in obsolescence, since it only has a licence for five years. Since it was created in 2009, the tenor of public opinion (hardened by talk of cuts and an age of austerity) has made the Olympic Park look a little less like a national triumph and a little more like a white elephant. Perhaps once it's over we should reverse the view, and offer tourists the chance to scale the obsolete stadia of the Olympic Park, then to gaze back in wonder at the 'Greenway', the northern sewer's answer to the 'Ridgeway', with its Lycra-clad cycle commuters pelting past signposts fashioned from old sewer pipes.

*

Britain's water companies are getting wise to the possibilities of tourism, and not just from avid birders. Few of us visit power stations to understand how our electricity gets to the sockets behind the TV, but now water companies have tapped in to our unslaked thirst for new weekend attractions to create picturesque edgelands visitor centres near reservoirs. So the residents of conurbations can spend a Sunday afternoon walking around their drinking water, then take a cup of tea made with it, while watching audio-visual displays to show how it all works. Tittesworth Reservoir in Staffordshire exemplifies this. It is, in itself, a beautiful place full of water birds, set amid the Staffordshire moorlands and visible from the Roaches. But the visitor centre run by Severn Trent Water shows the good burghers of the north Midlands – Stoke-on-Trent and Leek in particular – the hows, whys and wherefores of their drinking water. In ten years' time we may all be taking the grandchildren round the local sewage farm, to learn more about the other end of the plumbing cycle, then playing with the touch-screen displays showing the journey from toilet to tap and back again. Mind you, we might steer clear of the café.

Wire

The edgelands are a cross-hatch of wire. Because so few people live here, these areas lend themselves to an underground and aerial tracery of aluminium, copper and glass-fibre threads bearing voices, digits, voltage and hum into and out of the city. But at eye-level the pattern is more complex. These tracts of land are a bewildering mixture of high and low security. Here, where a Victorian mill has collapsed under decades of rain, the single strand of wire is less a fence and more a threshold, to mark out for kids where their territory starts. Years of crossing have given this wire a permanent sag, as if cowed by its own weight. But next door to this ruin is a freight depot, where juggernauts reverse into bays to be filled. Here the fences tower above you: double-weave steel sheets to keep you out. The edgelands are a complex mix of fiercely guarded private ground and common land by default, or by neglect. And the history of these places is held in their wires.

When you first encounter chain-link fences, as a child, they are better than ladders. With hundreds of snug-fit footholds, you can climb a fence of any height, at any point, with the crossover at the top the only moment of challenge. England's edgelands often function as illicit playgrounds for children, which explains why chain-link alone is rarely enough for an edgelands fence. Variations on the theme of fence include rows of upstanding spears tilted at the top to point outwards at potential climbers, plus the alternative toppings of barbed wire or razor wire.

Coils of barbed wire, like a well-trained bramble coiled along the top of a fence, are threatening enough, but razor wire takes latent violence to a new level. Kids at school who carried razor blades were unhinged, off-the-scale, unpredictable. Knives could get confiscated, were hard to hide. But a razor blade with tape on one side to make a handle, that could be tucked into a jacket pocket. Brandished once or twice, just the rumour of the razor blade would then suffice. At moments of confrontation, a hand in the relevant pocket would be enough to say 'Back off!'

Perhaps this is why, for young men, fences with razor wire provoke particular terror. It's a boyhood memory of that tricky moment when you swing one leg over the chain-link fence and try to get a foothold on the other side. For precious moments, as you make the transition, your crown jewels are inches from agony. Add razor blades to that already tense manoeuvre and you have a powerful deterrent.

*

Deterrence was a word familiar to any child growing up in the Seventies and Eighties. This was the official justification for the siting of nuclear weapons on British soil. Most contentious of all these sites was Greenham Common, in the edgelands of Newbury, Berkshire. Newbury had battlefields before, where some of the bloodiest clashes of the English Civil War were played out, but Greenham Common became a byword for apocalyptic threat, night-chills, the particular surreal horrors of the Cold War.

A whole generation of British schoolchildren grew up swapping stories about radiation poisoning, nuclear epicentres and the range and power of various missiles. There was a mixture of bravado and anxiety in this, as we tried to outdo each other's scare stories. But for kids brought up on the housing estates around Greenham Common there was an added edge. Not only did they know that they were living half a mile away from the Soviet Union's number one nuclear target in Britain, but they were also witness to the local (but internationally reported) daily and weekly battles between the US Air Force and the women protesters in the peace camps. And their battleground was a fence.

When the kids from the estates got jobs and bought their first clapped-out cars, they would head straight up to Greenham Common. The road that traced the outside of the base offered a decent challenge for a young driver, laid out as it was with slow bends and hairpins, dips and rises, long, enticing straights. But that wasn't all it offered. After a few minutes, a USAF police car would arrive and shadow you from inside the fence, matching your speed, slowing when you slowed, turning when you turned. If you stopped, they stopped. If you reversed, they reversed. This dance went on as long as you stayed by the fence. They looked at you, and you looked at them. They wanted you to know you were being watched. There was no spoken threat. After all, it was a public road. The threat was latent, but powerful, not unlike the threat of the base itself.

*

Many early computers ran on what was known as 'magnetic core memory'. This was, effectively, a tightly woven sheet of chain-link fencing, with multiple fine wires threaded through the rings. These old sheets of memory are objects of beauty in themselves, worthy of hanging on gallery walls, and their weaving was a skilled job. As magnetic core became the dominant form of RAM in the late Fifties and early Sixties, Scandinavian seamstresses and out-of-work Lancashire textile workers were enlisted to hand-weave these chain-mail memories.

So when a fence is taken down, like the fences around Greenham Common, rolled up like wallpaper to take away, what memories are stored in them? For those who believe that walls of old buildings can hold 'recordings' of sounds from the past, a metal fence could be equally plausible. And some of those memories are visible, tangible. Sections of the Greenham Common fence had ribbons and tokens tied to them as prayers or declarations.

*

Can disused military bases be considered edgelands? In one sense, their wire perimeters meant it was almost impossible to get anywhere near any actual bunkers or hangars. It wasn't a case of anybody not seeing them for looking, more a careful disposal of global forces that we weren't meant to look at. But since the Cold War thawed, and these places have been mothballed, it is possible now to get closer to this decommissioned landscape.

For his project *The Hush House*, the photographer Frank Watson did just that. Working like an archaeologist of the recent past around Cambridgeshire, Suffolk and Norfolk, he has meticulously photographed these once-forbidden bases. His images have the cool, analytical stillness of Bernd and Hilla Becher's studies of our industrial landscape, a recording of empty runways, vacated hangars, strange mounds with monolithic concrete entranceways that seem to recall both the post-war housing estate and the Neolithic earthwork, and wire, always wire. Empty of people, these spaces stand as still as the cornfields which now grow around them, rusting and overgrown, with wild flowers making confident stands in the cracks of pavements.

Might there come a moment when our descendants look upon these desolate fortifications in the same way we might visit a hill fort or castle? English Heritage has already produced a major study (*Cold War: Building for Nuclear Confrontation, 1946–1989*) and the huge, heavy structures aren't going anywhere. History has passed them by, moving on and leaving them stranded and inert under drizzly English skies.

In the meantime, site-specific theatre has moved in, along with the pioneer weeds. *Bentwater Roads* was a play produced by the Eastern Angles theatre company on the site of the former RAF Bentwaters. The base has a hush house – a room for testing jet engines with an exhaust port at one end – and the production made maximum use of its dead acoustic, an anechoic chamber where voices could carry over distance without amplification. From these inner sanctums, utterly unknowable only a few years ago, an unfocused dread leaked into all of our lives like a background hum. Now art is happening in their empty spaces.

*

In the suburbs and edgelands of many towns and cities now, fences are made to bear the most painful memories. Grief was once confined to graveyards, churches, to quiet corners in the homes of the bereaved. Now it has broken out, and 'roadside tributes' to victims of road accidents are so common we barely notice them any more. Some are temporary: bunches of flowers tied to a fence until the rain rots them off it. But some are tended like graves, visited, treasured. Now, it's not unusual to see photographs of the lost loved ones, laminated or printed on to plastic for weatherproofing. Some of these are poster-sized.

When Bolton Council tried to put a time limit on these roadside shrines, they were faced with street protests. The council had proposed a window of thirty days after an accident, when the outpouring of grief could be allowed to take its course. After that, the fence would be cleared, and teddies, photographs and other votive offerings could be collected by the family.

This was all predicated on the creation of a permanent tree memorial in a nearby park, to honour the victims of road accidents in the town. But for those grieving relatives, a memorial is not the point. The place is the point. They want the act of remembrance to be rooted in the place where their son, sister, mother, friend last drew breath, took a final fateful step off the kerb.

Gardens

What kind of plants and flowers do lorry drivers like to look at? Consulting engineers Sir Owen Williams and Partners, charged with the task of designing and planning aspects of the initial sections of the M1 in the mid-Fifties, came up with a proposal. Because Newport Pagnell Services were intended to serve the needs of primarily the working-class, male haulier and goods driver, a planting scheme was designed that would be in keeping with the tastes of proto-white-van-man: the central areas would be full of laburnum or thorn, these being 'in keeping with the necessity for attracting and pleasing the average lorry driver who would perhaps be more stimulated by a mixture of this nature than with the commoner ash/elm mixtures'.

There is an archaeology of attitudes to class and pastoral to be found growing at the sides of our major roads. Driving along the M1 motorway today is to travel down a long historical garden, the product of competing landscaping ideologies. Even though we like our English landscapes to be foxed and burnished with age and rich in historical associations, raw functionality and utility has its histories, too. The rampant horticulturalism of the Roads Beautifying Association, who might, given half the chance, have planted a long ribbon of forsythia and garden shrubs along the entire central reservation, superseded by the Landscape Advisory Committee's massed, functional plantings of primarily indigenous species, designed to be appreciated at speed, to improve the shape of motorway banks and the appearance of bridges. Landscape consultants vied with the Royal Forestry Society for England and Wales, arguing over the use of Austrian pines, copper beech, purple sycamore and whitebeam.

*

This overlooked landscape of road verges has begun to attract artists. The painter Edward Chell has been drawn to its inaccessible wilderness, mundane and sublime in its infinity. Chell first noticed how rich a landscape this is, like many of us, while inching forward in gridlocked traffic. Motorway verges today are pesticide-free strips of wilderness, as difficult to reach as sea cliffs, miniature landscapes that run along this in-between space for thousands of miles. He works from photographs and sketches, but access is difficult and dangerous: these are forbidden zones, places where the traffic police will pick you up within minutes. Working on the M2 and M20, Chell learned how to make himself invisible by wearing a hi-vis jerkin and hardhat: the twenty-first-century *en plein air* artist in disguise.

The paintings he produces suggest the busy-ness and fecundity of roadside verges, rich and alive. He has described the powerful visual metaphor of the verge as poised between the ordered, policed and restricted boundary spaces of the state that we are only allowed to look at travelling at great speed, and the slower, uncontrollable energies of nature. Working in shellac, he is also able to suggest a strange patina, what he describes as 'a kind of shot quality' (which brings to mind T. S. Eliot's 'flowers that are looked at' in *Four Quartets*). They suggest our perception in flux: the way, seen at speed, the intricacies of grassland and vegetation shift in and out of focus as our relation to the incident light changes. Because Chell is interested in vision, how we look at (or don't look at) what lies all around us. His paintings concentrate our gaze on what's usually fleeting and reduced to blurred texture; at the same time, their stillness seems to contain speed, and its shifting effects of light.

His attention extends to where his work is exhibited. For the work made at Cobham Slip and Maidstone Services, Chell decided the Little Chefs of Kent would make the ideal gallery, a place where the motorist, fresh from the experience of passing through corridors of grass verge, could contemplate these spaces. Working on the A66 and M6 for his Cumbrian project, Chell used the Little Chefs of Lakeland, not least because they also represent the equivalent of the old staging posts along the coaching routes (the Little Chef at Appleby is on the same road the Wordsworths used on their visits to north-east England).

*

Well-maintained public spaces, parks and playing fields and promenades, are not edgelands; but with a little neglect and abandonment they can become edgelands. A garden is vegetation under control, plant life held in various states of ecological arrest. Our sense of what a garden can be has long been contested, but perhaps a crucial turning point came in the eighteenth century. Gardens took European landscape painting as a key source, and at the same time there were also many advocates for a new wildness in garden design, offsetting the overly formal schema that, up until then, was popular. Alexander Pope wrote: 'In all, let nature never be forgot . . . Consult the genius of the place.' Pope's contemporary, the landscape designer William Kent, blurred the boundary. Horace Walpole, in a famous statement, declared that Kent was 'born with a genius to strike out a great system from the twilight of imperfect essays. He leaped the fence and saw that all of nature was a garden.'

In *Rubbish Theory* – Michael Thompson's investigation into consumption, cultural categories and the metaphysics of waste – a long-standing paradox is examined. If all of nature really were a garden, then interrogating Walpole's ghost would lead us up the garden path. If we asked him what fence did Kent jump, he'd tell us the garden fence, out of the garden into nature. But how can he have jumped out of the garden and into the garden? Why was there a fence in the first place?

Thompson describes the eighteenth-century landscape garden as a kind of conceptual artwork built upon this paradox. Beyond pure idea, the physical durability of this kind of garden is constantly under threat, and its existence relies upon control and management. Isn't this a strange contradiction we've been living with ever since? Landscape design has been contested ever since, too, but fragments of the English Elysium and old-fashioned picturesqueness lie all around us, especially in or near places where people actually work and live. It is palpable in public parkland, but its effects can still be seen and felt everywhere in our housing estates and business parks (even the language suggests a kind of stewardship of space), right down to the planting scheme on a roundabout.

*

The idea of the *locus amoenus* – the place of clement and balanced climate favoured by the gods themselves – has haunted the way English landscape has been viewed. This is the well-known 'demi-paradise' and 'blessed plot' of Shakespeare's *Richard II*, and the Albion of his contemporary, Michael Drayton:

> Where heate kills not the cold, nor cold expels the heat,
> The calmes too mildly small, nor winds too roughly great,

Nor night doth hinder day, nor day the night doth wrong,
The Summer not too short, the Winter not too long . . .

The English landscape most of us pass through now is a landscape of speed and displacement. The Areas of Outstanding Natural Beauty and National Parks might be our destinations, and these are managed, georgic places, where much hard work and effort maintains an ecological balance. However, true pastoral is more likely to be found in the edgelands, where our slipstream has created a zone of inattention. Here, even plants and animals meant to live oceans apart are finding their point of balance in the overlooked landscape we flash by in the blink of an eye.

There was a great fear of modern speed. Early railway travellers were anxious of the effects that those new velocities might have on their bodies, and it was speculated that cows in fields nearby a passing train would have their milk turned black. Even the long-distance horse coaches were considered dangerous: after completing the 400-mile journey to Edinburgh, Lord Campbell wrote how he had been 'gravely advised to stay a day at York, as several passengers who had gone through without stopping died of apoplexy from the rapidity of the motion'.

Now, speed is our element, and a new overlooked landscape has established itself. Left alone long enough, it would, in its own time, begin to efface us if we were to stand still. Near where the A34 crosses the West Coast main line south-east of Stafford, and only yards from the big grey retail sheds of Pets at Home, Next and Matalan, a caravan in a back garden is almost completely submerged in deep overgrowth. We like to clock this as we pass through the Midlands heading north, though like many other passengers it has taken us years of looking out of the window to learn to anticipate its passing and notice it.

How many other demobilised objects must lie out there, swallowed by each summer's new growth?

*

Does all managed urban green space aspire to the condition of an eighteenth-century landscape garden? It still seems to be the default setting. A new university has extended its campus and built extra student residences around its southern perimeter. The road network feeding into and out of campus has been changed completely: new roundabouts have been built, parking space extended. The immediate aftermath was the usual messy by-product of modern construction work: raw earth, disturbed land, deep pools of rainwater forming, hazard tape in tatters like bunting the day after a party. But day by day, visitors to the university could watch as plant machinery began to marshal the ground itself, shaping big rolling verges, smoothing over the cratered ground using rubble as infill and compacting it with a topsoil finish. Saplings were planted in diamond patterns, lashed to stakes or set inside short lengths of plastic drainpipe. Then, one day, a haze of green was just visible over the raw earth: the first shoots of sown grass, breaking through.

Gardens come to the end of their managed lives every day, too. A garden need only cross a notional line, or 'tipping point' to use a phrase made popular during this decade. The point at which species begin to take full advantage of our unconcern might also be the point where many long and well-tended aesthetic sensibilities are challenged. This is also the point at which the pejorative rhetoric usually kicks in.

*

The railway embankment has largely escaped landscaping. From a train entering a city, the rows of domestic back gardens abutting the railway have a familiar kludge of fencing, corrugated iron, doors and particleboard that marks the boundary between one kind of space and another. Escapees are common, seeds finding their way into a new corridor of opportunity, and blown along the tracks by the timetabled movement of trains. The verges easily slip into the category of edgelands. The view from the houses is shielded by all kinds of ad hoc screening, and rows of tall leylandii are attempts to block out the noise of the passing trains; at the same time, the passive rail passengers' view is mobile, a continuous fleeting panorama, and, even if they lift their heads from books or crosswords, they are unlikely to dwell on details. The result: a space that nobody takes much responsibility for.

And so brambles and bindweed form a kind of slow-motion surf, rolling down the banks into the cutting. In winter, the snarled detritus of the decades is clearly visible, lost footballs and unspooled video-cassette tape, tin cans and plastics of every description, tangled and suspended. Maybe a glacier is a better way of thinking about railway embankments. The litter from both back gardens and train windows is caught like till in the ice, inching slowly towards earth with the general tumble of each season's growth.

*

The ability of rail to offer you a new perspective on the overlooked, abandoned edges of a city is part of the reason it has inspired so many poets. Philip Larkin's 'The Whitsun Weddings' captures this beautifully. His poem describes the 'frail travelling coincidence' of a rail journey down the east of England one Whit Saturday in the late Fifties, when station after station the train doors open on to fag ends of wedding parties, and 'fresh couples' are ushered on board to begin their new life together.

From the start of the poem's journey, Larkin evokes that particular 'reverse view' you get from a train, passing through cities patterned on roads: 'We ran / Behind the backs of houses, crossed a street / Of blinding windscreens, smelt the fish-dock.' The poet tries to lose himself in a book, but his eye is drawn to the weddings and the changing landscape as the train approaches London, 'shuffling gouts of steam':

> Now fields were building-plots, and poplars cast
> Long shadows over major roads, and for
> Some fifty minutes, that in time would seem
>
> Just long enough to settle hats and say
>   *I nearly died,*
> A dozen marriages got under way.
> They watched the landscape, sitting side by side
> – An Odeon went past, a cooling tower,
> And someone running up to bowl – and none
> Thought of the others they would never meet
> Or how their lives would all contain this hour.
> I thought of London spread out in the sun,
> Its postal districts packed like squares of wheat.

*

Trains afford us the best views of allotments, a secret landscape often invisible from our main roads. Allotments signal that you are now passing through the edgelands as emphatically as a sewage works or a power station. They thrive on the fringes, the in-between spaces; on land left over (or left behind) by the tides of building and industrial development, in pockets behind houses or factories, and in ribbons along the trackbeds of railways. In the last century, the former train companies were one of the major providers of allotments – either for their own employees, or rented out in a wider disposal – so what the rail traveller today is seeing are the remnants of a private world, and a history of common land use.

Allotments have suffered from an image problem. Following the publication of a major report into their use and future, commissioned by the Wilson government in the Sixties, they might have been called 'leisure gardens', but the new name never really took root in the popular imagination. Seen from the train, they seem to hark back towards feudal, swineherd England, subsistence strips for the poor outside the pasture land and deer parks. They are gardens that make no secret of their physics and chemistry, blowsily revealing an infrastructure of water butts and pipework, all the ad hoc plastic groundsheets and carpet offcuts. They flaunt their functionality; the domestic garden with its hands dirty, busy and raddled with agriculture's businesslike clutter. They don't fit in. Minutes after leaving a central station, and the privatised shiny surfaces of the city, and there they lie, a cobbling together, like a refugee camp for those fleeing consumerism.

Where 'allotment' suggests something begrudgingly parcelled up and doled out, 'leisure gardens' might have reminded us that allotments were, in the eighteenth century, largely the province of the middle classes, and many English towns had belts of 'guinea gardens', small cultivated areas where flowers and kitchen crops could be grown, wells could be dug, and even a small summer house might be erected. Later in the nineteenth century, allotments were created for the urban poor, originally as charitable initiatives, then as part of local authority provision. They became working-class landscapes, engines of a hidden economy of exchange and reciprocity, a crucial if largely unacknowledged means of getting by. People grew their leeks and potatoes and carrots and beans to help support themselves, but also to give or to sell, in the communal hope that the favour would be returned, especially in times of glut. One view – in this case expressed by George Monbiot in the *Guardian* – contends that the general provision of allotments has been appeasing the poor for hundreds of years:

> Allotments have been used as a sop to the dispossessed for at least four centuries. The General Enclosure Act of 1845 took 615,000 acres from the poor and gave them 2,200 acres of allotments in return. Just because we love and value allotments, it should not stop us from seeing that they also represent paternalistic tokenism.

They continue to exist on a borderline between recreation and utility, and during the last century oscillated between huge popularity, as during wartime we were encouraged to 'Dig for Victory' on the home front, and decline, when many plots were abandoned and either redeveloped or left to return to nature.

The huge growth of interest and participation in public gardens and community orchards, together with the way that food ethics and a concern for sustainability and responsibly sourced product have entered the cultural mainstream in recent years, means allotments have become popular again, even cool, their promise of self-sufficiency, thrift and health coinciding with a broadsheet emphasis on environmentalism and what a PhD student somewhere is probably referring to as 'narratives of eco-catastrophe'. More visible than ever before, our world's wasteful scale and entropy baffles and paralyses us, but we can concentrate on the local, the immediate, and devote our attention to a few square feet of earth. They offer an alternative to a life of getting and spending.

Allotments slowly move out of the edgelands, even into the floodlit and shiny regions of media attention. They feature in food-porn shoots ('my tomato has been off the vine less than a minute, and travelled only three feet between plant and frying pan'). Even the most stylish of rehabilitations – a photo shoot for the shiny pages of *Vogue* or *Harper's Bazaar* – doesn't seem at all far-fetched any more. Charged with working in a context so far removed from conventional glamour, stylists would relish the challenge to make mulch and horticultural fleece seem desirable. The waiting lists have grown long again. Gaining membership, and a plot, can be a complicated and long-winded process in popular areas. In some cases, it would be easier to join the Garrick Club.

Though a moving window might provide many of us with our best views of allotments, we need to get off the train to really experience what's going on. Taking a closer look from on the ground, we open the old iron gate and walk through the network of pathways, past the steaming compost heaps and pockmarked braziers, the shanty town of sheds, the latticework of beanpoles and canes . . .

*

The village of Wolverton in Buckinghamshire has long been submerged by the great gridwork of space station Milton Keynes, which might help explain the pockets of resistance to be found here: within a relatively small area you'll find a secret garden by the railway (on the site of the old stationmaster's house, behind the Electrolux factory), a community orchard, and plenty of allotments. If Milton Keynes is a city made out of roundabouts, then Wolverton is its allotment district, a former railway town blessed with irrepressible plots and sheds.

The strangest sheds you might encounter on a walk around this allotmentopolis are those converted from railway carriages. From their windows the view is static, only changing as the seasons turn through the landscape. We imagine a journey stalled for decades on the outskirts of a town, our business and destination long forgotten, the inscrutable, tortoise-burying gardeners coming and going, ageing slowly from the window of one of these simple time machines.

*

If we think of allotments as places for masculine retreat and sanctuary, then allotment sheds are their inner sanctums, the poor man's safety-deposit box and reliquary. In theory, they can be inspected at any time, but they are a good place to stash and hoard, away from the prying eyes of wives, children and the police. Some are strung with hammocks, or have tubular steel camp beds folded away in corners: quiet places to sleep one off. Among the onions drying on a shelf sits an unreported skull, its teeth still grouted with the clay it was clad with when somebody dug it from the ground several springs ago. Loose teeth rattle in old seed packets. Back runs of *Practical Woodworker* and *Carpworld* lie fallow, looked at, mined and worked out. Heavy old desks that once sat in studies suffer a strange afterlife in the paraffin gloom, a vice clamped to their lips, their deep drawers stained with purplish permanganate. Some are cluttered with relics from the hands-on world: drill bits and puncture-repair tins and set squares and spark plugs and bobbins of fuse wire. Another contains wintering dahlia tubers, dusted with sulphur powder and wrapped in newspaper. In a chest of drawers a Luger with its firing pin removed lies wrapped in an oily tea towel, though Yeats' 'The Lake Isle of Innisfree' is still just legible. On top of it, a four-gallon plastic keg still contains the dregs of last summer's harvest bitter, the owner's contribution to the home-brew ring that operates on these allotments. Lying alongside this might be a two-stroke motorcycle engine block, in pieces, a mockery of the neat exploded view in the Haynes manual that lies open beside it.

Outwardly, the allotment shed must often conform to all manner of strict codes of appearance and build, depending on council and society. But, tempered to local and immediate needs, infinite variations on a simple theme can be encountered, making the allotment shed a homespun equivalent to the sonnet or the concerto: circumscribed by general rules, but forced into all manner of individual invention and in some cases decoration. Position, size, building materials, even colour and finish might be preordained, but within these parameters anything might happen in the hands of a master shed-builder. Even the canonical pre-constructed sheds seen hanging from wire caging at DIY superstores and garden centres can be subsumed to local tradition and personal predilection.

Maybe the real gardens of the edgelands are the polytunnel plantations, the tomato- and strawberry-forcing factories where hectares of land are kept under polythene. They extend the English growing season, and allay the amount of imported soft fruits needed to satisfy demand, but are unpopular because of their appearance: a plasticky visual blight. England under wraps.

*

Heading north out of Oxford towards Port Meadow, we pass along the riverside path and admire the rich allotment-land on the opposite bank. It's an overcast day in early March, and the motley of sheds draw menacingly close to the water's edge, reflecting darkly in its zinc surface, and even seem to sink their rootstock into the riverbank itself, which is shored up with sheets of corrugated iron and wooden switch piles.

Do sheds lead a double life? The artist Simon Starling might have us believe so. In 2005 Starling made *Shedboatshed*: scouting around the newly refurbished Kunstmuseum in Basel, the artist had discovered a big shed at Schweizerhalle on the Rhine a few miles upstream, and set about deconstructing it to make a *weidling*, a kind of local riverboat, which he was then able to punt back downstream to the gallery, where it was dismantled, rebuilt and displayed as a shed again. That autumn, *Shedboatshed* was displayed at the Tate in London, and won Starling the Turner Prize.

In among all the other lumber inside each of these sheds off Binsey Lane, there is always a paddle. They are prepared for when the water levels rise here. When the rains fall for days, the people will come, and begin to break their sheds apart, reassembling them on the waterlogged clay, a mass transformation of rickety wood, old planks and weatherboard: the opposite of flat-pack. Braziers will be fired; the damp air will sweeten with the smell of pitch being used to caulk the seams of these new vessels. The larger craft – amalgams of two, sometimes three sheds – get fitted out with primitive tarpaulin sail rigs. Others are much smaller, closer to currachs or coracles. But come the allotted time, the whole shambolic, improbable shed fleet will take to the water and sail silently away in search of firmer ground for growing leeks.

*

Perhaps it is a function of economic recession, but 'Dig for Victory' is creeping back. That famous slogan is no longer used, of course. Both 'victory' and the implied nationalism are complex ideas now. There are moments of clarity, like those sad and remarkable funeral processions through the streets of Wootton Bassett, when we still glimpse what it might mean to do something 'for' our country. But now the call on our conscience is primarily to act for the good of the whole world.

'Dig for Planet Earth' seems to be the implied slogan behind the drive to grow our own produce, to 'Think Globally, Act Locally', to turn over as much wasted or underused land as possible to the beauty and utility of growing fresh fruit and vegetables. This is an international phenomenon, and the Urban Farming Movement is one of its founders. It was established as a response to the grinding poverty of inner-city Detroit. As the economic tide drew out, parts of the city were virtually abandoned to crime, despair and decay. So in 2005 'Urban Farming' was established, to bring people together to cultivate waste ground, rooftops, industrial ruins, lost spaces all over inner-city Detroit, and to make those spaces fruitful.

Each harvest is shared out, free, for the hungry. Neighbours are encouraged to contribute produce to 'food banks' that will seek out and help the very poorest. Urban Farming is a major success story, spreading in its first five years to develop over 800 new urban gardens in the United States and abroad.

*

The English Pennine town of Todmorden may not be twinned with Detroit, but the same imperative to grow good local food has taken hold here. Todmorden's 'Incredible Edible' began by developing small public herb gardens on the verges of the Burnley Road, or in planters on Todmorden railway station, where commuters were encouraged to pick a sprig of local herbs as they waited for a train. Now, like the Detroit venture, 'Incredible Edible' has taken off, and has built extensive links with local government, health authorities and schools. Its ambitions now stretch to orchards, fish farms and locally produced eggs.

*

A future fast approaches in which – after the second world recession of 2020 puts some of Britain's best-known high-street brands (the ones that survived in 2009) out of business – Britain's homemakers send their kids after school to gather the ingredients for their tea from the shared gardens in the old ruined factory, the railway sidings, the grass verges of the East Lancs Road. Then on the way home, they grab a handful of herbs from the beds outside the picturesque ruin that once was Tesco Metro, and dash back for a locally produced feast.

Lofts

Pigeons are the edgelands angels of the north. Anyone travelling on the train line that runs from Newcastle to the Metro Centre in Gateshead might have noticed the pigeon lofts built along parts of the trackside. As you pass through Teams and Dunston, they rise up out of the brambles and bindweed, ramshackle sheds built from old doors, corrugated iron, offcuts of timber, pallets, anything the builders could get their hands on. No sooner has the traveller's eye tuned in to their recycled shapes and textures passing by – no two seemingly alike – than they're gone again. But for a few moments there was a glimpse into something like the medieval, or the developing world, a few minutes from the largest shopping centre in Europe, a shanty ribbon development of tumbledown huts.

They call them crees up here: crees, from the creosote used to proof and season them. Coops might be acceptable, but only posh people have lofts. The pigeons are bred and trained for racing; the north-east of England is a stronghold of pigeon fancying – this is the home of the Up North Combine, the West Durham Amalgamation – though the sport is in a long slow decline. Birds find their way home over great distances, a feat that many of their owners find moving. These birds are a quantum leap from Woody Allen's 'rats with wings': good pigeons regularly change hands for hundreds, even thousands of pounds, and are fed with special corn and vitamins. Each club member has a clock that is synchronised with the club's master clock, and the birds are released at a set time from the sides of basket trucks hundreds of miles away from their lofts. A bird's arrival back at its loft is clocked, and speed is calculated by dividing the distance between race start and loft with the time taken.

It's a long-standing hobby, often seeming closer to a devotion or even obsession (tales of wives feeling neglected by husbands spending long hours in their lofts are legion), embedded into the edges of this region, linking the present to a largely vanished culture of collieries and pit men. It can also be a deadly serious business. Lofts have often been burned down here, full of roosting pigeons. Birds have even been kidnapped.

Wedged between the railway lines and the streets of terraced housing, the crees are one way in which the shed has evolved, a place where men can go to immerse themselves in a little universe outside of and parallel to their lives. In the air above the streets here, the clap and pulse of a batch of pigeons turning circuits is part of the texture of the everyday. The pigeon fancier sits in his cree on a Saturday afternoon with *Sports Report* on the radio, hidden away in the edgelands where nobody comes or cares, but his birds fly where they may. They are emblems of space, of an untrammelled imagination, and the pleasure of watching the clock while waiting for them to return home to such a secret place must be a kind of paradise.

Canals

Anyone who has worked on London Underground will tell you that there are 'ghost' stations in between the living ones. British Museum, Down Street, Brill, Lords, York Road, some of the names are oddly familiar, and some of the platforms are almost untouched, with intact billboards advertising long-forgotten products. If you press your face to the train window and peer into the darkness, and if you know where to look, you can get a flash of the past as the station pelts by.

To get an equivalent glimpse of the past in England's edgelands, a canal boat may be your best bet. When TV documentaries examine economic decline, they often put a camera on a narrow boat. Cue moody cross-fades: smoke-stained walls with smashed windows, blocked chimneys sprouting trees between their bricks, seized-up pulleys. Once the economic equivalent of our motorway network, the canals are uniquely able to offer a portrait of the decline in manufacturing, and the shift of power from water and rail to road. Of course, the canal networks are long and varied, cutting through open countryside, city centres and gentrified estates. The way they negotiate changes in height, their locks and lifts, their vertiginous bridges and aqueducts, all are testimony to this miracle of Victorian engineering. But canals do offer a glimpse of our Victorian past, and of what we have done with it.

*

Our canals now lead a double life. Where they cut through the countryside, they have been adopted as 'natural features', barely distinguishable from rivers. In fact, their tranquillity and association with pleasure-boating gives them the edge over rivers for many weekend walkers. Where they turn urban, it's a different story. Here, canals are wet skips, fit for dumping anything and everything. These two kinds of canal meet in the edgelands, where a dog-walker might pause, a little anxiously, as his dog sniffs a graffitied warehouse wall, and gaze along the towpath as the walls give way to open wasteland.

So stark is this double life that you wonder what their future might look like. How can this broken network – once the backbone of the world's most industrialised nation – be reconnected and revived? One answer may be gentrification. Many and varied are the balconied canalside apartments and floating restaurants emerging from dark stretches of our urban waterways. And then there is the romance of narrowboat life. Just as the ancient frost fairs allowed for revelry and licentiousness, because the law of the land did not extend to frozen lakes and rivers, so life on a canal seems to offer an escape from convention and restriction. Walk past a mooring and your eye is drawn behind the lace curtains, where couples who have dodged the rat race wave to you, their matching bicycles strapped to the deck of the garishly painted *Lady of Shallot*, kettle whistling on the stove, and an open copy of *The Wild Places* on the table. Now, across England's canal network, boat-hire companies let you taste this reverie for anything from half a day to a fortnight. Once you pay your money, a young man ushers you on to your boat, and teaches you to drive by tearing (well, chugging) to the nearest bridge, where he hands you the tiller and leaps ashore, leaving you to steer an unfeasibly long vessel through an equally unfeasibly small gap. Whatever tranquillity the canal-dwellers have found is hard-earned.

But there are other visions for England's canals. In a recent report by the think tank Demos – 'Resilient Places' – its authors, Samuel Jones and Melissa Dean, suggested that the future could lie in commerce as much as leisure.

The Demos report points out that the canals – the dotcoms of the nineteenth century – are perfectly placed for the revolutions of the twenty-first century. Run-down or gentrified, our canal network offers a unique set of connections between towns, cities and villages, and a truly national digital network requires a truly national geographical network. 'At the time of writing,' say Jones and Dean, 'five hundred miles of fibre-optics are buried beneath Britain's towpaths, connecting city to city, company to company, community to community.'

England's manufacturing power has gone, perhaps for good. But there is a poetic justice in the idea that the same network – Aire and Calder, Coalport, Grand Union, Grand Western, Kennet and Avon, Leeds and Liverpool, and on, and on – that shipped our raw materials and goods in the nineteenth century looks set to ship our raw materials and goods in the twenty-first. Only now the cargo is information, and it ships at the speed of light.

And light is not the only commodity handled by our reborn canals. They take heat too. According to British Waterways, the west London headquarters of pharmaceutical giant GlaxoSmithKline now dissipates one megawatt of heat into their local canal. The employment of canals to cool and heat buildings is another part of their reinvention.

*

The Bridgewater Canal is orange. This is one of the key facts about canals learned by any north-west schoolchild for more than two centuries. Its distinctive colour comes not from modern pollution, but from ancient iron salts in the local rock. This canal was completed in 1776 to take coal from the Duke of Bridgewater's mines into the growing industrial furnace that was Manchester. Some local guidebooks described it as 'ochre', which is probably more correct, but for a schoolchild this was the orange canal. Its colour was sufficiently striking for a boy to agree to a walk along the canal at Worsley with his grandparents, despite the paralysis that usually seizes any sane child on mention of a 'walk'. While the adults pointed out the fancy houses of the footballers (usually wrong, it turns out, as Lou Macari can't have lived in all six houses at the same time), we kids would gaze at the river, conjuring as we did so dreams of rivers of melted chocolate orange.

Imagine then, our horror, as we learned of a £2.5 million scheme to 'clean up' the Bridgewater Canal. Apparently, the 'ochre' deposits inhibit the growth of flora and fauna. We are sure that this will lead to a wealth of fish leading happy lives in the waters of this beautiful canal, and that future reluctant children forced on walks will admire those fish in the crystal-clear waters, as well as looking for footballers' houses. But it won't be the same. It won't be orange, and we will not be going back.

*

There are other businesses along Wolverhampton's canal banks: car-body shops, small engineering firms, a complex of 'banqueting rooms' to rent for parties, weddings, works outings. But the ebb tide of the heavy industries can still be heard, like the swash over pebbles as the waves draw back. It has been said that the impressive record of the English Midlands in producing heavy-metal bands is down to the likes of Black Sabbath, Rainbow and half of Led

Zeppelin being brought up to the sound of the car industry, the real heavy-metal sound of the bodyworks, as sheets of steel were stamped and hammered into shape by vast machines. Metal as the poltergeist of heavy industry. So as you walk (or even, heaven forfend, jog) the canal banks of Wolverhampton today, you should ensure there is a heavy-metal soundtrack on your iPod.

★

Many of us who were raised near canals can remember a winter or two when the water seized up and you could walk on it. This was a risky business, but there was always one kid who would chance it, step out gingerly on to the striated edges where the ice met the grass bank, and then half skate, half run to the other side.

Once on the other side, and once the whoops and cheers died down, the kid who crossed the frozen water either had to muster enough courage to do it again, or – cowed by stories of cracking noises, sure that luck would not protect for two runs – make the long solo walk on the other side to find a bridge or lock to cross to get back to his friends.

And there was always the fear that you might not find a way back over, that there was no proper towpath on the other side because no one's meant to be there, that the unfamiliar side would keep you there as darkness fell: marooned, between the uncertain ice you dare not cross twice, and the safe landscape of the other side.

★

The edgelands can provide a range of surreal culinary experiences: eating chips while waiting for your kill-tally to flash on the screen at Laser Quest, or buying a bag of hot chestnuts from a man in Victorian garb outside a factory outlet. But Jabula is up there with

121

the best of them. This South African restaurant is situated next to the Cheshire Oaks retail park near Ellesmere Port. Here, you can munch a piece of crocodile, kudu, ostrich or springbok at a window table as a massive cargo ship passes on the Manchester Ship Canal right alongside you, like a total eclipse of the sun, on the Bushveld, only the sun is a big ship, and the veld is Ellesmere Port.

Bridges

Nameless bridge, its cast concrete walls and pillars are dark with run-off stains and vertical deltas of algae. It carries a minor road across six lanes of motorway, and nobody is ever meant to really look at any of this. It is a barely registered, blink-of-an-eye space; the grass verges have turned to stone here, forming inhospitable ramparts to either flank of its span. Only a trauma – in the form of a Monday-morning suicide, or a payload of breeze block dropped into the fast lane – can draw any attention to it, and even then the wound of disruption seems to seal itself over quickly. It might easily fall back into being a nameless bridge again.

This kind of bridge doesn't suggest any great triumph of engineering. Here, the man-made isn't traversing a great estuary or deep valley, with all the confidence, swagger and aplomb of an earlier age: it is doing its job, a tone poem to absolute function and utility, dead loads and live loads, longitudinal forces and wind. It is unimpressive but lapidary. The edgelands are full of bridges just like it, carrying smaller roads or raising the motorway itself across back lanes, canals and byways.

Somebody has been here, though: there is graffiti. The nearer the bridge is to a major city, the greater the chance of finding that florid aerosol-work we associate with urban train yards and rail sidings. The allegiances of its football fans are declared in plainer script, a change in invective indicating some invisible boundary has been crossed and new waters entered. Graffiti is part of the visual noise of our age, in the same way as broadsheet ballads once supplied the background buzz of earlier centuries, and is perfect for the mobile gaze; the short, emphatic, florid statement of name, protest or allegiance, an impression meant to be made at high speed.

The most sought after aspect of any bridge graffiti has to be the overhang: a territorial claim, insult or obscenity could be registered by millions of motorists who pass under it. Somebody has risked life and limb to compose a message in letters as high as those found on the prow of a liner, or the screened credits of a Hollywood movie. Working quickly and awkwardly, and with the ingenuity of a prone fresco painter on his scaffolding, they have declared to the passing world that MANCS RULE, or SCOUSERS DIE.

*

Over time, a bridge graffito becomes a de facto milestone. Our motorways are signed with the familiar white-on-blue Transport lettering of distances and directions, but unofficial eruptions of words serve just as well to mark our journeys, to tell us how far we've come and how much yet lies ahead of us. Graffiti often takes a long time to fade, especially so if remote and inaccessible, and many revetments and overhangs and piers still carry the ghostly messages and invocations from the recent past. REAGAN CAN STICK HIS CRUISE MISSILES UP HIS ARSE. WE WON'T PAY POLL TAX. LES GROOVES DOGS' BOTTIES. Not all messages are meant to be as pointedly adversarial or shaming, though. Sometime in the Nineties, the first GOURANGAs began to appear. For a time, these messages, carefully fly-posted out of individual letter panels, were mystifying and difficult to read. Were they the work of viral marketeers, pushing a new brand of health drink? Who, or what, was this Gouranga? It slowly became clear that these were happy-advocating bulletins from the Krishna movement, prompting an even stranger image of bands of monks at work in the English land-scape, armed only with wallpaper paste and a good head for heights. Some of their work persists to this day.

*

Some texts on bridges were never meant to last. These are the greet-ings and felicitations daubed on strips of torn white sheets, tied to a bridge on the commuter route of GILLIAN, she of the 40 YEARS YOUNG TODAY message, or HAPPY BIRTHDAY DAVE THOMAS 21 TODAY!

Occasionally, these bed-sheet bulletins are public declarations of private feelings: TRACEY M WILL YOU MARRY ME? or SALLY P LOVES DANNY J. And a temporary bridge sign is a good way of delivering a spoiler too. Many parents can remember one fateful morning finding the home-made banner DUMBLEDORE DIES stretched out across the M6 in full view of their sleepy children. This was mere hours after watching TV news pictures of kids queuing at midnight outside bookshops to get a copy of the latest Potter tome. It is tempting to imagine a struggling children's author, sick with jealousy over the young wizard's success, queuing for one of the first copies, flicking to the end to see who dies, then heading out in darkness to the M6 with a freshly daubed sheet.

And what happens to these messages? As the rain soaks into them, the heavy cloth droops and the painted letters smudge. Perhaps the more public-spirited bed-sheet artists come back – when the birthday is over – and cut their banner down, rolling it up to take home. Others are removed for safety's sake. After all, no one wants their windscreen blanked out by a sodden CONGRATULATIONS SANDY dropping from the bridge above.

*

If you're looking for signs of pioneering architectural work on our motorways, then all roads lead to the M1. This is the site of our first motorway bridges, many of which are still in use, and they were designed by Sir Owen Williams, his son Owen Tudor Williams, and his partner Robert Vandy towards the end of the Fifties. They were built using concrete to a standardised spec, allowing for local variations in span, height, width and skew, and they were not liked. Basil Spence – architect of Coventry Cathedral – did compare their strength and span to some of the great Roman works, but mostly these bridges were panned. They were seen as ugly, brutal, cheap, coarse, anti-aesthetic, a disruptive check on – and an impediment to – the fluidity and sense of easy flow the motorway should have engendered. The poet John Betjeman thought they were 'matters of lasting regret'.

*

Who uses motorway bridges? Well, herds of cows do sometimes, on their way from field to field, heads down, oblivious to the screaming rush beneath them. TV news reporters do, when illustrating bank holiday traffic jams or interviewing junior transport ministers. Infamously, some kids use them to launch bricks and rocks at windscreens.

But there are simpler pleasures to be relished here. As young children, we had to cross busy roads like the East Lancs to get to the sweet shop on the other side. This used to involve holding the hand of an adult, and waiting for traffic lights to let you cross to the halfway island, then (in a separate light change) on to the other side.

And then one summer the bridge came. It was blue metal, with a surface like sandpaper to stop you slipping. Now we kids could cross on our own, and we took ages. Every giant's footstep we took reverberated through the whole bridge with a deep, loud boom. We would stand directly over the fast lane, watching the cars undercut us, waiting for the HGVs. They were the best kicks, the tallest lorries swooping under you, mere inches below your feet.

*

Far and away from our conurbations, on the lonelier northern stretches of the M6 or the M5 south of Bristol, bridges stand plain and quiet, too remote to gather the excrescences of language. These bridges are like islands or reefs, gathering a little of what the tide of traffic brings: lost hubcaps, the barley sugar of broken indicator glass, an elemental, technological-iron-grey dust that seems to accumulate in the road kerb as a by-product of speed and flux, and discarded tachographs. These last are perhaps the most mysterious of roadside items: little waxed paper wheels divided into twenty-four segments, the offices of long-distance haulage, they resemble astrological charts plotting distance and time between remote objects (say, Stevenage and Sandbach Services). Sitting in the gloomy crook of one of their internal angles, these bridges can feel as isolated as any hilltop or windswept trig point, the passing pulses of traffic making a similar echoing roar to the swell around a sea stack or cave.

*

Road-combing, we sometimes came across pieces of cardboard blown into the hollows beneath bridge piers, or turning mushy in the pyracanthas on the edges of service station slip roads, each one carrying a handwritten scrap of language. These are the desired destinations of hitchhikers – L'POOL, ABER'TH, MK, J33, CAMBS, M6, PENZ – written in bold black marker pen (the hitcher's friend) and forgotten and discarded at the ends of journeys completed or aborted (or the beginnings of those attempted but never made). We made half-hearted attempts to collect these found objects. They reminded us of Dylan's 'Subterranean Homesick Blues' from the movie Don't Look Back (if Dylan had plundered a UK road atlas gazetteer), cue cards meant to be read in the split-seconds of the passing motorist.

In 2000 the photographer Chris Coekin decided to travel the length and breadth of the country by hitching, taking pictures of his journeys along the way. It began earlier, and in Germany, when Coekin and his fellow traveller the Big Fella – self-styled 'hitching virgins' – had attempted to cross Europe at the mercy of 'The Road', and Coekin described that peculiar combination of self-consciousness and anxiety caused by sticking a thumb out to oncoming traffic. The project he set in motion back in the UK subtly adjusted the relationship between subject and photographer: Coekin was a very different kind of documentary artist, one invited into the spaces and lives of his subjects by their shutter-quick decision to pull over and offer him a ride. He photographed himself – in car parks, in lay-bys, on grass verges – using the camera's self-timer, and he also turned his lens on to the human debris and roadkill collected in the camber and grassy margins. The project works as a kind of travelogue, drawing on elements of documentary, portraiture and still lifes, with Coekin at the centre of his own road movie.

*

The poet Jean Sprackland has a sequence of poems about the East Lancs Road. More specifically, her poems are responses to the detritus thrown or dropped from cars and washed up on the shores of the central reservation. In collaboration with the photographer David Walker, she produced a sequence of poems called 'No Man's Land'. These are poems about the objects marooned in the middle of this busy road, but also the people connected with those objects:

> The rag-and-bone man would give away a balloon
> in exchange for a broken saucepan
> or a coat riddled by moths.
> My mum boiled the bones clean for soup first
> and kept the best rags for the floor.
>
> There's no currency mean enough round here
> for trading in ring-pulls and plastic bottles,
> the loops that hold beer cans together,
> the polystyrene panels a fridge comes packed in.
>
> You can buy a roll of fifty black sacks for a pound.
> They hang flapping in trees and no one bothers to free them.

*

Rail routes, carrying their passive, captive audiences, are punctuated by station names and nothing much more beyond topography and landmarks. But commuters slowly learn how to recognise and time their journeys by their particular corridors of graffiti activity. Individual tag artists – and, even before Banksy, many deserved to be called artists – acquire a kind of infamy, especially those who venture far out of the city. Their industry and commitment is admirable. In Brighton, DEAN became a legend. The road bridges, blind gable-ends and walls leading out of the city, through Preston Park, read like a long sentence of the same proper noun, endlessly varied in its tone and colour but always recognisably the work of one hand and never any more or less than the simple statement: DEAN. Once the London line tunnels into the huge natural barrier of the South Downs, one might expect occurrences of DEAN to come to a halt, though this isn't what has happened. DEAN continues north beyond Burgess Hill, extending far into the Sussex Weald on junction boxes and signposts, rising above the litter-choked surf of brambles: the most unexpected and inspired sighting comes to those passengers who notice how even a metal cattle trough in a field almost halfway to London has been bombed: DEAN.

*

In his 'Poems on the Naming of Places', Wordsworth draws the link between person or event and topography. Anonymous edge-land bridges sometimes find a name will stick, and sometimes a whole history and mythology, too. Perhaps the best exemplar of this is to be found in those rich, bracing edgelands of the West Midlands that lie between Wolverhampton and Birmingham New Street. As the train runs close to the Old Main Line canal near Oldbury Junction, a small bridge can be glimpsed crossing the water bearing the simple and stark words TOJO THE DWARF. The bridge itself has outlived the station it once served, and its name on the old OS map of the area – Union Furnace Bridge – has fallen into disuse, because in these parts, this is known as the Tojo Bridge.

Who was Tojo? Mere mention of his name provokes a smile of recognition from many West Midlanders. There are rumours of a

Tojo's Bridge Appreciation Society. Many theories have been put forward to explain the graffito and identify Tojo; there have been calls to have a sample of the paint analysed and dated. There is something unresolved in the baldness of the statement, painted boldly and without embellishment with what might be ordinary household gloss: its meaning tips between public insult and a kind of existential declaration, depending on the viewer's mood and proclivity. He must have been many things to the daydreaming rail passengers who have passed by, a figment of their imaginative landscapes: a scapegoat who has never shown his face around these parts again, or a short figure surveying his work then gliding away in his black vaporetto through locks that must lead eventually down to open sea.

*

Not many of us, queuing on the M5 to join the M6, will have thought too hard about what lies beneath. Most drivers are fixed only on the landmarks that afford them some (however forlorn) sense of progress through the Midlands bottleneck – the iconic Dunlop building, the muscular, futuristic shapes of the electricity sub-station, the RAC Control Centre jutting out over the traffic like the prow of a flagship.

But underneath this long, extended bridge, this complex of flyovers, is another world. This is the world of Tarkovsky's dystopian film Stalker: dark, damp, intense and menacing. Peel off the flyover and circle round to get at the edgelands below. There you take a turn into one of the many industrial estates dotted along the motorway. Follow a looping road through the estate and you meet a dead end, blocked by tall fences and razor wire.

We park the car and peer through the fences. Those fences are twice our height, tall metal stakes drawn to a point. Signs all along say that crossing or climbing is forbidden. No one must go in there. So we press our faces to the fence, and we see the River Tame, a Styx in semi-darkness mirroring the journey of the flyover above. They seem organically connected, with a thousand steady strings of drips falling from the rain-drenched road above, to break the surface of the canal. It is as if we can see inside the body of a road, its viscera, its bloodstream.

*

On the West Coast railway line heading south to London, edge-lands bridges play an important role. Of course, they still do what they have always done; the sudden pressure changes, shifting the background key of the train on the track, but they also now compli-cate the lives of busy people.

Not long after you pass the massive McVitie's factory in Harlesden on a morning train south – take a deep breath to see if you can smell baking biscuits – the bridges start to come at you. At first, they come and go quite swiftly, unnoticed by most passen-gers. We are fast approaching London. Meetings are imminent. Business is pressing.

'Yes, I understand that, John. But I told you . . . Yes I did tell you we needed the mock-ups by Tuesday . . . Yes I did . . . I know you can't plan for things like that, but you did have plenty of notice . . .'

Then the bridges get wider and darker, until on the last ten minutes of the journey (what one guard on the tannoy memorably called 'our final descent into Euston') the bridges seem to merge into a series of long tunnels with brief glimpses of light in between. John's lament about the mock-ups splinters into syllables, then gutters out.

Masts

Now, wireless transmissions are so complex and commonplace we take them for granted. The sculptor Marilene Oliver in a striking piece called *Text Me* made a sculpture of a human torso being impaled from every direction with words from text messages and e-mails, in short sentences like crossbow darts, reminding us that other people's words, images and information are passing through us all the time.

And it's the fear of the effect of these waves on our bodies – founded or unfounded – that makes the siting of masts and transmitters such a controversial issue, which is why so many of them end up in the edgelands, where schools and homes are rare, and few people are likely to raise objections. Here's an edgelands spiritual exercise. Head for the scrubland outside Big Storage or the B&Q Warehouse, where the pallets rise like a fortress over the razor-wire fence. Stand like a latter-day St Sebastian, and open yourself to the multiple text messages, wireless e-mails and mobile phone calls cutting through you. Sift through the trivia, the cold calls and spam, until you reach the desperate evocations of love, loss, fear. Listen to them whisper as they pass through you. Take on the cares of the world.

*

We live with a steady bombardment of radio waves, and move through the zones of macrocells (antennae found high above the height of an area's surrounding structures, bolted to masts or rooftops), microcells (found on streets: physically blended into the colours and shapes of brand names and logos above shop windows) and picocells (often found inside buildings, especially where demand is high such as train stations or malls). There are now so many that a demand has arisen for hiding antennae. And it's become possible to blend these devices into the visual texture.

A chimney stack on a listed building can shroud a telecoms device. The skills of set- and prop-makers for the film and TV industry have migrated into the everyday to provide realistic brickwork, complete with moss and algae. Telecoms concealment is all around us. Perhaps the biggest breakthrough to total coverage – part of the war against black spots and signal edges – would mean the development of living cells. Rats of course would be the obvious choice for research and development: they live in the silent tunnels and move through the crawlspaces of the most confined and patchy interstices of our cities. Everyone knows how you're never more than a few feet from a rat.

*

Never less than accommodating, the edgelands have helped to ease our anxieties about mobile phone transmitters. After all, if you can't see them, you are less likely to worry about them. So some mobile masts are now masquerading as trees.

Wander out of an edgelands hypermarket car park into a belt of scrub woodland, and you might notice one tree that doesn't quite fit. It is perhaps a little too uniformly greenish-brown, a little too smooth in shape. But these disguises can be so convincing that birds and squirrels are fooled, so you probably won't know if you see it.

Known in the trade as 'stealth towers', these undercover trans-mitters call to mind that familiar TV comedy trope (see *Monty*

Python, 'Allo 'Allo, Dad's Army, etc.) in which soldiers are disguised as trees or bushes to ensure a surprise attack on the enemy. And trees aren't the only costumes in their wardrobe. They can do a pretty convincing flagpole, too, and in America the rooftop crosses of some churches now send two messages at once – salvation and telecommunication.

*

Electricity pylons find their true home in the edgelands. In towns, they worry people. Whatever the scientific evidence for or against negative health effects from high-voltage cables, their sheer size and lethal power make them unpopular neighbours. In the country-side, they are regarded as an eyesore. A necessary evil, perhaps, but unpopular just the same as they stride across valleys breaking the landscape's clean lines. Only in the edgelands do these giants look at home, with their sagging skipping ropes and the ominous crackle and hum as you approach them.

Drawn to their majesty and beauty, the photographer Simon Denison decided to make images of their footings with a pin hole camera. The pin hole produces tenebrous close-ups, illicit and mysterious, of the meeting of steel foot, concrete base and uncut grass. Denison's work inspired a collaboration with the poet Philip Gross, who shared his fascination for these towering figures with their feet firmly planted in the edgelands:

> . . . the planetary module, million-
> dollar-sweet metallic kit,
> wakes up to find itself
> bedded down in a red grit desert.

Wasteland

We arrived at Prescot in Knowsley with just an hour or so before darkness set in, an overcast English evening sometime between the run on Northern Rock and the Cadbury's takeover. We soon found a huge open space near the railway, where the Cables Retail Park has gained a small foothold, offering the usual high-street chains, a supermarket and abstract concourse sculpture. Prescot was for a long time the home of British Insulated Callender's Cables, and a huge operation that manufactured copper cabling connecting up the pre-digital, pre-optical world. It has all gone.

In living memory, the streets of Prescot and the surrounding area, where the street lights are all just pinking into life, must still contain a great neural network of clocking-on times, repetitive tasks and scheduling, all the intricate routines and rhythms of the working day: BICC, up until fairly recently, was the local employer. But all that physically remains of this now, at the centre of it all, is a vast void. The factory floors have become a wasteland of stones and rubble, and the production lines that once paid out incalculable millions of miles of ocean cable have themselves turned into a bare seabed.

It's an uncanny openness. Most of our cities will contain several sites just like this, either lying completely fallow or in the process of being redeveloped. It's always a surprise, walking along a busy city street, to find a gap in the shiny advertising hoardings or a bent-back sheet of corrugated iron which affords a view on to an open wasteland carpeted with flowers in summer, or the archaeological earthworks of new building work where foundations are being laid. The city, suddenly, has a new scale, an underness and overness, and the eye, having scarcely a moment to readjust from the enclosing streets and buildings, is overwhelmed. The journey to a high moor or heath in search of wilderness and communion with nature involves a slow readjustment in terms of scale and space, but a city wasteland is all the more mysterious for the manner of our encounter with it: the imagination does the travelling. As if alert to the value of the spectacle, some contractors now cut small square windows into the shield of their hoardings.

*

Adam Buddle could be described as one of the chief architects of England's edgelands. Except that he wasn't an architect at all, but a botanist who died 300 years ago. But he did (courtesy of Linnaeus) lend his name to a plant imported from South America, a plant that has with the help of wind and weather, self-seeded across huge swathes of unchecked, uncultivated land around our towns and cities.

The buddleia or 'butterfly bush' has become such a significant marker of edgelands territory, that 'kingdom of buddleia' is not a bad name for the largest stretches of these purple flowers, on large, open wastelands like the huge stands behind the hoardings of Albion Street just outside the centre of Wolverhampton.

And that vivid purple is a perfect complement to that other dominant edgelands tone, the deep red-brown colour of rust. At its most painterly, this combination can be found where huge rust-coloured gas holders rise out of the purple jungle, and passers-by admire the beauty while holding their breath.

*

Our urban wastelands can penetrate into the hearts of cities, though they are most often encountered on their edges. These areas can be extensive, though nothing like as widespread as the Zone that once surrounded Paris. The July Monarchy of the French 1840s had cleared a space, forbidding building and erecting fortifications in a ring around the city, the Zone itself being a strip of land 250 metres wide operating as a glacis, or firing zone. Like a woodland fort where the tree cover has been cleared to the range of a rifle shot, the city's *banlieue* stopped at the edge of an open space that, by the end of the century, had become occupied by squatters, gypsies and rag-pickers, outcasts living in an illegal shanty town. They called it *la Zone*, and its occupants were known as *zoniers*. They built a city within a city, a network of streets and passages, populated by *apaches*, the lower-class gangs feared by the bourgeois, and the *chiffoniers* of Baudelaire and Benjamin. They spoke their own argot.

By the end of the First World War this populous Zone was obsolete and the government set about dismantling it, using a compulsory purchase order to take it out of military hands and develop it, though the *zoniers* were so long established and settled in their separateness that they hung on for several more decades, until the Zone was obliterated by new cheap housing and the building of the huge *boulevard périphérique* highway that encircles the city to this day.

English wastelands, mosaics of former industrial sites and brownfield land, have occasionally served as home to gypsies, who are forced to live out of sight in quiet pockets beyond the city's suburbs, though such a purposeful belt of wilderness, populated by its own demi-monde, has never girdled any of our inner cities. Today, the new Zones might be those inner-urban areas skirted by CCTV and surveillance technology: the City of London's 'ring of steel' uses eight entry points equipped with cameras linked to the Automatic Number Plate Recognition System, a digital, medieval, city-gate network. Drivers' faces are recorded and stored on a database. The new Zone relies on fibre optics rather than the firebreak land of the City of Light.

*

The Prescot cableworks once had a war memorial on a wall near the factory gates, a familiar bronze tablet turned to verdigris, listing the names of all the employees of the British Insulated & Helsby Cables (as it then was) who had fallen in the Great War. This memorial is now kept in storage by Knowsley Council, and looking over the flattened site in the dusk, it's easy to wonder whether this is probably the factory's largest surviving artefact. Nobody has figured out a way of remembering any of this yet. In the wide-open emptiness and absence, the eye starts to pick over the debris for tiny clues and fragments.

*

Known chiefly as a war photographer, Don McCullin is also one of the greatest artists of our cities' wastelands. Powerful black-and-white images from the Sixties and Seventies show Bradford, Doncaster, Consett, Birmingham, often with a single figure pitched against the landscape, resolute against the grey skies.

One image, part of a sequence taken in Liverpool 8 in 1961, features two young boys, about ten years old, standing on a classic piece of wasteland, strewn with bricks, stones, abandoned cars and bits of industrial machinery. A row of houses stands in the background, some smashed and empty, though one still has painted window frames and curtains. One boy looks across at the camera, straight at us, but the other is coiled backwards like a longbow at full draw, blurred with speed. He has a stone in his hand. This could be one of many traditional wasteland games: throwing stones at bottles, throwing stones at windows, throwing stones at passers-by. But such is the strength of his backward arch that his stone will fly over the bottle, over the coal yard, out of the wasteland, out of Liverpool to drop in the icy shallows of the Irish Sea.

*

Recession is good for wasteland. If any cleared terrain is left unmanaged and ignored, a natural order of succession is allowed to run its course. Firstly, the pioneer species arrive, blow-ins like rye grass and ragwort and rosebay willowherb. Seeds cadge a lift in the tread of earthmovers and lorries, or arrive from the air in birdshit. Knotgrass, white clover, and what the poet Derek Mahon called 'the earth-inheriting dandelions' might also make their presence felt. The ecologist and lichenologist Oliver Lathe Gilbert described how many early colonisers – wormwood and mugwort, willowherbs, Jacob's ladder, knotgrass, cinquefoils, docks – seem typical of what might have been found during the late-glacial period, suggesting that conditions on wasteland must have many similarities to those that existed following the end of the last ice age, and wondered if 'a number of the species may never have had it so good since'.

There then follows a tall herb stage, featuring competitive longer stemmed varieties, followed in turn by grasses. Looking at a decade old patch of wasteland, you might typically be seeing a thick sward of grassland, broken by taller clumps of herbs, though the earlier, successional stages can still be 'read' in the great variety of species still persisting. If the wasteland is left undeveloped for longer, woody plants might find a way to assert themselves. Goat willow, common willow, birch, ash, sycamore, broom, hawthorn, elder and brambles might all dig in for the long haul. What you typically end up with is scrub woodland.

Wasteland weeds and flowers are as individual to the twenty-first-century English city as a forgotten coat of arms or motto. By the Eighties, Gilbert had surveyed many of England's wastelands and urban demolition sites, and noticed all manner of regional variations in their plant life. He even thought it would be possible to accurately place a town in its regional setting following a careful look at the flora found on its waste ground. The north/south divide in terms of summer temperatures controls the buddleia, which flourishes in the south, but gets scarcer as you head north. An east/west climate gradient, where cloudiness and rainfall increase the further west you travel, affects plants like hogweed and creeping thistle, which prefer the drier eastern coast. Then local soil plays its part, and historical human activity needs to be considered, too. The combination of all these factors results in specific local plant environments where indigenous and invasive species thrive side by side, forming a local identity completely at odds with the creeping homogeneity of the high street.

*

Bristol was a buddleia city (Gilbert reported a graffito that read: BUDDLEIA RULES OK!), succeeded by sycamore; traveller's joy was doing well, red valerian too, and there were naturalised fig trees on the banks of the Avon. There are branches of Starbucks, Carphone Warehouse, WH Smith, Dixons, Currys and McDonald's. Further west, and over the border, Swansea was dominated by Japanese knotweed (where it is known as rhubarb or cemetery weed), and had much buddleia, hemp agrimony and pale toadflax; there was also red bartsia, silverweed, sea campion, buck's-horn plantain, polypody and ivy-leaved toadflax. There are branches of Starbucks, Carphone Warehouse, WH Smith, Dixons, Currys and McDonald's. Sheffield featured many garden escapees, blooming from June through to October in a succession of feverfew and goat's rue, tansy, soapwort and Michaelmas daisies. Pink-, purple- and white-flowered goat's rue covered the hillsides, and eastern rocket, wormwood and Yorkshire fog did well. There are branches of Starbucks, Carphone Warehouse, WH Smith, Dixons, Currys and McDonald's. Liverpool had many early successor populations of yellow crucifers, lesser-hop trefoil, black medick, wall barley and melilots; hedge woundwort, cut-leaved cranesbill and evening primrose also flourished. There are branches of Starbucks, Carphone Warehouse, WH Smith, Dixons, Currys and McDonald's. Manchester had Japanese knotweed and giant knotweed, while reed grass and other wetland species did well. There are branches of Starbucks, Carphone Warehouse, WH Smith, Dixons, Currys and McDonald's. Swindon supported extensive stands of St John's wort, with wild carrot, wild parsnip, welted thistle, great burnet, crow garlic and ploughman's spikenard. There are branches of Starbucks, Carphone Warehouse, WH Smith, Dixons, Currys and McDonald's. Hull had a variety of creeping thistle, spear thistle, rosebay, willowherb, docks, goosegrass and ox-eye daisy. There are branches of Starbucks, Carphone Warehouse, WH Smith, Dixons, Currys and McDonald's. Birmingham was all about golden-rod and larger bindweed. There are branches of Starbucks, Carphone Warehouse, WH Smith, Dixons, Currys and McDonald's.

*

Urban wasteland hermits, supported by start-up grants and seed-corn funding, setting up in business, entrepreneurial herbalists. In Germany, where the culture of the health spa still flourishes, there is a spa for every ailment and malady: a spa for the lungs, a spa for heart disease, a spa for testicular trouble. Whole towns are devoted to the treatment of one thing. Imagine, then, visiting an English city's wastelands for the specific attentions of its specialist hermits. After studying and reviving ancient texts such as the *Materia Medica*, the great herbals of the Germans Fuchs and Gresner, the *Discorsi* of Matthiolus, and the English herbalist John Gerard, it might be possible to make a living foraging for simples among the rubble and ruins of an abandoned brickworks or factory, along the verges of dismantled railways, and in acres of vacant city-centre land awaiting redevelopment.

*

Picture this: on a swathe of post-industrial wasteland near the Lawley Middleway, just to the east of Birmingham city centre, a licensed hermit is collecting golden-rod. Over a pallet fire he makes his golden-rod tea, which is good for sore throats, coughs, colds and flu.

Another hermit is a familiar sight gathering toadflax through the summer months along the roadsides, railway tracks and brownfield sites in and around Swindon. Later, behind an advertising hoarding on the A419, he prepares an infusion to be used as a purgative liver-cleansing agent, or boils the plants up in lard to make a green ointment that is excellent for piles and skin eruptions.

A hermit well known in Wolverhampton makes his home in the ruins of a goods yard near the canal, hidden from view by the vast stands of buddleia; he hunts for wormwood and mugwort during long early walks around the area's hardstanding ground, both of which have many medicinal uses, but his speciality is skullcap, found on walls next to the canal itself, brewed into a mild sedative decoction.

*

After eradicating all his worldly goods as foreman and destruction-line overseer of Break Down, the artist Michael Landy might have easily become something of an ascetic, a hermit. Left with only the clothes he was standing in, Landy must have wondered whether starting all over again was an option: in the long aftermath of Break Down, he was reported to have worn clothes given to him by fellow artists and friends.

He turned his attention to weeds, seeking out the overlooked and neglected vegetation to be found growing through the cracks in the pavement, at the margins of car parks, on waste ground, collecting them carefully before taking them back to his studio to tend. He then spent long hours over an etching plate making highly detailed, life-sized images of these 'street flowers'.

The resultant prints, collected as a series called Nourishment, resemble botanical illustrations – the flower, leaves, stem and root-stock are all meticulously recorded as a single isolate plant and presented like specimens – and we're struck by the concentration lavished on the groundsel, Canadian fleabane, herb robert, toad-flax, thale cress; the lowly, the blow-ins, the survivors, the plants that survive in the slenderest of niches and cling on in our un-examined places. Each one reminds us of Yeats' 'befitting emblems of adversity', intricately and defiantly making do in our rubbish and neglect.

*

On a summer evening, stepping though a gap in the rusty corrugated iron and entering a well-established patch of wasteland is to enter an arbour of scents. As soon as wasteland has begun to collect pioneering plants, the insects follow, and where there are insects there are birds. As the order of succession and establishment continues, a site can become incredibly biodiverse and locally rich in species that find an ecological niche, an opportunity. The big threat now is redevelopment, and it's a substantial one. Some of these ecosystems might only survive for one season of growth.

Pressure groups and think tanks deplore the state of unused land and brownfield sites (often using the size of football pitches as an accessible analogy for the surface area wasted), and up until very recently the likeliest outcome would involve the dreaded landscaping: the occupying flora would be slashed and denuded, the surface either turfed over or spread with new topsoil and seeded with grasses. Old seeds can remain viable in the ground for years, though, and any slackening in management will see them rising again. But the goal here, the overwhelming urge, is to tidy up, to make everywhere look like a kind of pleasing-on-the-eye parkscape.

*

Roy Fisher's 'City' is in part an act of memory, but also an exercise in looking, and a portrait of the overlooked parts of his English midlands. As we travelled through Fisher country, we found evidence of the overlooked and the to-be-developed. Tracts of former industrial and living space have given way to the all-conquering buddleia, or are screened off with fences awaiting the agents of recreation or renewal. When recession strikes, places like this can atrophy. Architects struggle for contracts. Half-finished buildings are abandoned, waiting for the financial tide to come back in. Fisher calls these the 'lost streets':

> These lost streets are decaying only very slowly. The impacted lives of their inhabitants, the meaninglessness of news, the dead black of the chimney breasts, the conviction that the wind itself comes only from the next street, all wedge together to keep destruction out; to deflect the eye of the developer. And when destruction comes, it is total: the printed notices on the walls, block by block, a few doors left open at night, broken windows advancing down a street until fallen slates appear on the pavement and are not kicked away.

*

Edgelands beekeepers have been quick to spot an opportunity, often using hermits in the same way as the Kenyanese Boran people would use the greater honeyguide bird (which has one of the most magical binomials: *Indicator indicator*). The hives are situated within easy foraging range of good wasteland, in an unexposed, warm, airy setting; the bees waste no time in finding the huge brakes of buddleia on city-centre spoil heaps, the carpets of black medick on capped landfill, the rich corridors of railway embankments. The beekeepers look on admiringly as the workers waggle-dance their figure-of-eight routines, information-sharing and task-allocating in a language of space and movement that has no conception of *eyesore* or *wasteland*. The honeys they produce are far more multi-layered affairs than those obtained in rural areas, and the particular profile and scattering of an area's many wasteland nectar plants means a honey as tuned in to soil conditions and climate as any fine burgundy from a Côte d'Or *terroir*. The problem of pesticides is circumvented: unmanaged wasteland flowers tend to be truly wild and untreated. Edgelands honey is an organic product.

They sell it by the roadsides, in lay-bys, at catering kiosks. Near where the M42 and the A45 meet, just south-east of Birmingham International Airport and the National Exhibition Centre, beekeepers are advertising their produce to passing trade. Driving home from imaging expositions or clothes shows or doll's house events or antiques fairs or diabetes conferences, the curious pull over. The honey they find is full of deflected sweet-nesses, and those with a sensitive palate have reported how it is possible to discern, within the louder and more obvious notes of clover fields and bindweeds, a myriad of different species. They are tasting the waste meadows and verges built from soil heaps, the planting schemes of car parks and business parks, but because this whole area was once deciduous forest – Shakespeare's Forest of Arden in fact – they are also picking up fainter taste signals from the earth, its older seed store, the deep memory of place.

*

How can a pair of poets write about England's wastelands without at least a nod to T. S. Eliot? He was a poet of the city, albeit the 'unreal city', rather than the edgelands, but in *The Waste Land* there are glimpses of scenes that might bring a smile of recognition to an edgelands connoisseur:

A rat crept softly through the vegetation
Dragging its slimy belly on the bank
While I was fishing in the dull canal
On a winter evening round behind the gashouse
Musing upon the king my brother's wreck
And on the king my father's death before him.
White bodies naked on the low damp ground
And bones cast in a little low dry garret,
Rattled by the rat's foot only, year to year.

Between the wars, the idea of the wasteland seeped into British art like a brown fog. The disillusion and dereliction in Eliot's poem, first published in 1922, seemed to find its broken images reflected in the work of many artists and writers, though one of the most committed to the very real no-man's-land to be found on the edge of the urban and rural was the painter, photographer and collagist Julian Trevelyan. To Trevelyan, wastelands were rich and suggestive places.

A southerner by birth, well travelled and educated (he had studied art in Paris in the early Thirties and – an early indication of his predilection for wasteland – had spent time exploring and drawing the Zone in its waning years before it was redeveloped), by 1937 he found himself working for the Mass Observation movement, an anthropological research project founded by anthropologist Tom Harrisson, poet and reporter Charles Madge and documentary film-maker Humphrey Jennings. Untrained observers would keep detailed diaries of day-to-day life, record the anecdotal and over-heard, or answer questionnaires; artists would record by making work, and Trevelyan was assigned to the organisation's Worktown Project, a study of the community of Bolton.

He photographed a world of chimneys and rubbish heaps and rubble-strewn earth, of allotments and fences, the industrial dereliction where the people of Bolton ('Worktowners') existed, isolated figures moving through a desolate landscape or rummaging on tips. But his most striking work was made using collage. Using magazine cuttings, newsprint and paper, he recycled pieces of the ephemeral world to create images of the same dumps and pylon fields, standing pools and factories with their smoking chimneys. Trevelyan's wastelands are dynamic places, alive as a result of their indeterminacy; their fragments appear caught in a kind of unresolved tension. They suggest to us a new way of looking at an ignored landscape, neither grimy documentary realistic nor entirely whimsical and surreal, but occupying a border territory in between.

Ruins

Pieces of broken glass click underfoot. Every few paces, the floor becomes spongy with pads of mosses, until eventually you're standing on a hard and level surface. The air smells cold and musty, uncirculated, tinged with motor oil, mildew, brick dust, black unguents. Somewhere high above there's the ghost applause of a pigeon, before – a hundred yards or so in front of you – you hear the harsh metallic rattle of big shutters being rolled open. The screech of a car means you can feel the size of the echoing emptiness you're standing in; the engine draws near, nearer. Even though you're wearing a blindfold, you know this place. You've been inside here before many times.

*

The edgelands have a continuing role in British TV drama. Although this exposure keeps them in the public eye, their agent should be worried about typecasting. Every time the phone rings, it's the same role – denouement. Did it start with *The Sweeney* in the Seventies?

After all the lapel-grabbing, jaw-breaking, fast-talking, hard-drinking build-up, the final car chase streaks out of the city and into a vast open yard between disused warehouses and broken, red-brick ruins. Cars slew to a halt on the smashed up concrete stage punctured by thistles and willowherb. Doors slam, shots are fired. The chase is on foot now, inside the vast, empty warehouses. Here are abandoned offices to hide in, rafters to climb in, stacks of crates to push over. A man is shot, and his body drops from the roof beam. Or he is tied to a chair and beaten until he squeals. Or he opens a suitcase full of stolen banknotes, then they slam the cuffs on him.

As a rule the cops win, but if the writer is cut a bit of slack, crime sometimes pays on TV. Either way, one thing's for sure. The ruined warehouses of our edgelands are the losers every time. Even when they are not hosting the denouement, they are the madman's lair, the gang hideout, a place of unwitnessed assignation and assassination.

Of course, this is part of the appeal of edgelands for some. As the geographer Tim Edensor – a connoisseur of industrial ruins – says, these places often exist in a hiatus between the end of one industrial era and potential future redevelopment. As such, they become non-places, quite literally off the map – 'an impossible designation of space as terra nullius, which suggests they are spaces of and for nothing'. And they atrophy because their blood supply is cut off. As Edensor puts it, 'They have been bypassed by the flows of money, energy, people and traffic within which they were once enfolded.' But, of course, the apparently 'blank' status of edgelands industrial ruins opens up great possibilities for all kinds of licit and illicit pastimes, including the infamous trio – sex and drugs and rock 'n' roll. Well, okay, sex-and-drugs-and-rock-'n'-roll photo shoots.

*

You can have a vocation as a warehouseman. We met one on our travels. He was a quiet, tall man in his forties, propping up the bar of a brand-new edgelands pub. His story was all too common.

Credit crunch, fewer goods being shifted, warehouses emptying, staff laid off, warehouses abandoned, locked and left like huge empty hangars.

Our warehouseman had worked for a decade at the same warehouse, around the corner from the pub. In that time, he had handled books, CDs and DVDs, electronics, clothes. It made no difference. He was not there for the products. He was there for the warehouse, the space, the long straight aisles and the stacks of boxes. He loved the order and the structure of it, the stacking, the clean lines, the inventories.

What would he do now? He was at a loss. Signing on. Could not imagine any job that was not in a warehouse. Maybe, when the economy picks up, they will come and unlock the doors again, lorries will return and unload box after box. Then they will need warehousemen again. He will wait. It is his calling. He finishes his drink and ushers us outside. From the car park he points out a long, shallow, corrugated roof like a metal horizon over the scrubby edgelands trees. That was his warehouse. Now it feels like the empty church in Philip Larkin's 'Church Going': 'A shape less recognisable each week, / A purpose more obscure.'

*

Factories can pass from their original state of useful activity and be completely reinvented, while retaining many vestiges of their former identity. This was especially true during the property boom from the mid-Nineties onwards, when infirmaries and eye hospitals and depots and bra factories found themselves hollowed out and honeycombed with retail space or hotel rooms across the land. But one strange, hybrid way of redevelopment is the 'factory fascia' model. For decades, passengers to London travelling from the Midlands or the north-west have checked their watches by the 'Ovaltine clock' on the factory at Kings Langley, at the same time subconsciously registering that they are about to pass under the M25 and enter into metropolitan headspace. The factory is still there: or its front is. Behind the art deco façade are several hundred apartments. This is ruin as set design; the view from the passing train preserved.

*

Recent edgelands warehouses are clean-lined, brightly coloured, corrugated, but their beauty is only half the story. Alongside and between these new and bright big empty sheds are ruins. But these are no 'bare ruined choirs' photographed by tourists. No coach trips visit here, no information boards give you a drawing of these buildings in their heyday. No one paints them. Well, no one except mavericks like George Shaw and David Rayson. Yet they are romantic. If a romantic landscape is a place so atmospheric that it offers deracinated human beings a glimpse of the sublime, then edgelands ruins should be tourist magnets.

This would be a tourism like no other. As Tim Edensor describes it, these are dangerous, unpredictable places to walk:

> ... matter crumbling underfoot, the crunch of mortar and broken glass, and the feel of decaying matter. The body is apt to be buffeted by wind and rain, by gusts heavy with dust, and by atmospheres thick with the presence of damp. The relatively quiescent soundscape becomes a composite of lower-decibel murmurs, soft echoes, and scurries of unseen movement: the drips of water, eddies of winds, creaking machinery and doors, the cooing of pigeons and their flurries of urgent flight.

Similarly, ruined smellscapes are a heady brew of damp masonry, rotting wood and fungus, acrid chemicals, and the surprising bouquets of summer flowers.

Many modern edgelands warehouses – hit by the credit crunch – may be echoing shells, but the older ruins are far from empty. Their economic tide went out decades ago, but their shores are still full of fascinating detritus. For some aficionados there are rich pickings here. This is not beachcombing, but edgecombing. Tim Edensor lists some of his edge-combed treasures:

> . . . patents from the early 20th Century, old posters instructing workers in the art of safety or pin-ups of mid-century celebrities and sporting heroes, cigarette cards, a winter jacket and cap from the Baltic states . . . letters of complaint from customers and a brick bearing the label Utopia.

*

To walk in edgelands ruins is to feel absence and presence at the same time. Absence comes in the form of office chairs without office clerks to sit on them, ashtrays with cigarette butts stubbed out twenty years ago, newspapers breaking stories we have digested and forgotten.

In a disused bank in Cardiff's edgelands, pens still cling to chains on counters approached on all sides by damp and mould. On the other side of the counters, above each sheet of toughened glass, a sign says: Smile. Say 'Good Morning/Afternoon'. Say 'How can I help you Sir/Madam?' Why do those courtesies seem to be mocked now, by the smashed windows and the rotten floorboards? Didn't they know that at some point their bank would come to ruin? Birds flap noisily under the ceiling. The old counters are streaked with white. In the old bank manager's office, through a heavy oak door behind the counters, what looks like a wooden desk opens up to reveal a washbasin. We think of the manager, ushering out another disappointed would-be entrepreneur, shutting the door and washing away the sweat of a nervous handshake.

*

We are aware of how insistently we claim that edgelands are spaces in flux, often changing their character swiftly and without warning. But their transience really can bewilder. A few years ago it was possible to follow the lanes leading south from Heysham in Lancashire and come upon the wreck of an abandoned holiday camp at Middleton Sands. At the beginning of the Noughties the writer Michael Bracewell described finding its scarlet funnels and fittings taken from real liners, rusting quietly in the long grass:

> Reached through lanes of diminishing width; in early summer the dry green perfume of tall hedgerows, topped with a chemical note – the somehow archaic smell of Germolene – from a concealed works, beyond a steel fence. We don't know what they do there. You feel the land is coming to an end here, and it is.

We remember the smell, the porthole windows and the scabs of corrosion eaten into the once white walls, a coastal ruin redolent of old hit parades and full of the ghosts of holidaymakers from summers long past. We decide to go back, to see how the holiday camp is doing in its afterlife.

We can't find it. Places with names like Compression Road and Gas Field Road are grafted on to what feel like older, hedgerowed lanes. A newly built holiday retirement village lies at the end of one of these, all fresh tarmac and seeded earth verges. We were sure this was it. There is nobody at the gatehouse – the whole place is deserted – so we walk towards the sea, hoping to catch sight of a red funnel. It's a brisk day in early spring, and the fenced-off areas beyond the new homes are ominously filled with mounds of rubble in between papery dry stands of dead sedge and reeds. As we reach the shore, we find a car park next to a gym, and follow a recently lain tarmac path down to the shore that ends crudely and abruptly, like a lava flow into water. As beaches go, it's forlorn: the 'sands' here consist of a stony strand of reddish, sea-smoothed rubble, with all the attendant littoral detritus of plastics and glass. The sea is a long way out, and glassy mud stretches off into the distance. The ominous grey box of Heysham Power Station dominates the view north.

Back at the car park we find a man who appears to work at the retirement village, the first person we've seen here. 'Where's the old Pontin's holiday camp?' we ask him. 'You're standing in it' he says. We look into space, as if searching for the Crystal Palace or Field of the Cloth of Gold. All trace of it has gone, as if one day the building suddenly produced steam from its funnels and slid westwards into the sunset. He tells us how 3,000 people used to come here every week in the camp's heyday. Work on the new development now has stalled, slowed down and cooled off with the economic climate. But things will pick up. We wonder if any of the retirement villagers might be woken on washed-out August nights of wind and rain to hear the laughter of holidaymakers, their younger selves. And what of that smell, that chemical, faintly medicinal tinge?

An old ICI plant that made petroleum products. Gone. It's like visiting the ruin of a ruin.

*

The heritage industry tends to rely on a kind of freeze-framing of time in order to present the tourist and visitor with a reordered, partial, tidied-up account of what happened at any particular site. Edgelands ruins contain a collage of time, built up in layers of mould and pigeon shit, in the way a groundsel rises through a crack in a concrete floor open to the elements. They turn space inside out, in the way nature makes itself at home indoors, or in the way fly-tipping gathers at their former loading bays, behind obsolete walls. Encountering the decay and abandonment of these places is to be made more aware than ever that we are only passing through; that there is something much bigger than us.

*

Edgelands ruins are unpredictable terrain, full of ramps and pits, drops and cambers, open floors and tight corners. This makes them a skateboarder's paradise. One of the edgelands' defining sounds is the hum and rumble of boards, the emery scrape as they stop, the click as they lift off a kerb, the crack as they hit the deck.

But edgelands boarding has its own particular challenges, like nettle-beds. In the other world, nettles are mown or poisoned. In the edgelands, they flourish. Every child knows what it is to see the red weals rising on your arm or leg. But a skateboard can deliver you whole into a bed of them, and there are never enough dock leaves.

In towns and cities, skateboarding is encouraged and discouraged. Corners of playgrounds are fenced off, and metal ramps

157

installed. But as soon as the boards leave their compound – tempted by the lure of wide open spaces: car parks, shopping malls, the slopes and jumps offered by forecourts of office buildings – then they are moved on.

So they head for the edgelands. The same pattern applies in virtual boarding. The best of the skateboard games allow your avatar to go anywhere within a hybrid city. You can skate in the malls and the parks, you can knock down pedestrians, you can even skate down the middle of the road, smack into a car at full tilt, lie on the road splayed and groaning, then remount and carry on regardless. But even virtual skateboarders get moved on, by officious security guards and police.

So, you head for the virtual edgelands. And wow. The game designers have taken the best features to create fantasy skateparks full of huge concrete curves and bridges, complete with panoramic views as you lift off from the top of a multi-storey car park. The sun always shines here. The police never come. And no matter how far you fall, or how many times, you groan and get up, good as new. In one new game – *Shaun White Skateboarding* – you change the world as you skate. The better your boarding, the more the edgelands' utopian contours shape themselves around you, carving concrete into ramps and half-pipes.

*

Feral is the new wild. After all, what's so good about wild animals, wild flowers? All they do is what their instincts tell them, what their genes taught them. Feral means you have a history, a proper back-story. And the edgelands are the domain of the feral. Here, finding shelter in the old ruins and food in the overgrown wasteland outside, cats forget their pet names, swap the lap and the sofa for the pile of discarded overalls, or the car seat with its sporty trim.

The feral car seat is another emblem of edgelands. Every childhood should have one. In an age before computer games, sitting in one of these making engine noises was as close as a child could get to the open road. Or you could strap the car seat to a go-cart and find a slope. And you can rock them on their metal runners, survey your empire of feral knotweed, balsam, poppies and willowherb like an old hillbilly on a wooden veranda.

*

Why is there always an abandoned TV in the rubble? They are so ubiquitous in life that their bodies in death litter our wastelands and edgelands. And why does a dead TV's blank face resonate so much with us? Is this our image of oblivion? Now a TV should never be blank. There is no excuse. Gone are the days when – if you sat up beyond midnight – the credits would roll, anthems were played, and the stations were replaced by shash. No one sees shash now, but it was naked television. Shash was the term for those black-and-burst patterns that danced across the screen when there was nothing being broadcast. You could turn the lights off, and watch this electric snow dance across the room.

We are so preoccupied with what is on TV (or not on it) that we lose sight of the strangeness of the box itself. As Jean Baudrillard puts it, describing a TV set left on in an empty room: 'It is as if another planet is communicating with you. Suddenly the TV reveals itself for what it really is: a video of another world, ultimately addressed to no one at all, delivering its images indifferently, indifferent to its own messages.'

'There is nothing more mysterious,' Baudrillard concludes. And he's right, except that an abandoned TV on a heap of rubble at the edge of a city runs it pretty close. And the same goes for computer monitors. The late Irish poet John O'Donohue – who lived in a remote cottage in the west of Ireland – put his old computer monitor on the drystone wall at the end of his garden, looking back at the house. He did it, he said, 'to punish it'. So there it was, blank but evocative of pathos and longing, obstructing the view between the house and the mountains.

Woodlands

Brendon Chase is a classic of children's storytelling, written in the age of *Swallows and Amazons* by the cryptically named BB (real name Denys Watkins-Pitchford), who also illustrated the book with intricate woodcuts. Published in the Forties, it tells the story of three brothers whose parents live abroad, brought up by a frosty maiden aunt. It is the end of the Easter holiday, and the boys decide they don't want to go back to boarding school for another term. Instead, they run away into the local woodlands known as Brendon Chase.

What follows is an account of a year in hiding as the brothers turn feral in the woods, trapping and killing and fishing, fashioning their own clothes out of animal skins, evading capture. So, this is a book about public schoolboys and wildlife carnage. Not a fashionable recipe. As Philip Pullman concedes in an introduction to the republished work: 'Not only do they kill: they steal wild birds' eggs and catch butterflies, the rarer the better. To a modern sensibility, this is worse than advocating the compulsory use of hard drugs.' But despite all that, as Pullman says, this is a book 'brimming with delight'. And the source of that delight is more fashionable than ever.

Behind the Boy's Own adventure story, this is a book about human beings going back to nature – not just to 'the natural world', but to their own true nature, as creatures of the wild woods. But where are the wild woods now?

*

Our English woods are a complicated and sustaining myth. We yearn for traces of the original tracts of greenwood. We grow to understand that human activity in these islands had denuded the tree cover fairly significantly even during prehistory, but nonetheless we retain a strong imaginative attachment to our woods, especially as places for hiding and as places beyond the codes and authority of the day. The forest, even in the sense of a hunting ground, retains an idea of a region where different laws obtain, a place – etymologically accurately – *outside* of our everyday world. We look for what's left of Robin Hood's Sherwood, a few miles to the east of the M1 in Nottinghamshire. We want to find an Epping Forest in Essex that a fugitive Dick Turpin could hide out in. We imagine the lone copse surrounded by arable fields or the farmer's shelterbelt of woodland to be the last remnants of a primeval forest that once covered the land, green pools left over in the bed of a vast retreated inland sea.

'A culture is no better than its woods,' wrote W. H. Auden, and perhaps every culture gets the woods it deserves. Following the retreating glaciers of the last ice age, woods existed for a time unhindered by human interference; there then followed a period where humans cleared their spaces in the forest to farm and create land for grazing. We then used woods as pure material, the fuel and fabric of our existence, a process that accelerated our technological abilities, sustained our economies and underwrote our military capacities. Even by the sixteenth century there was a widely dispersed iron industry that (as well as its proximity to sources of ore) relied on a ready supply of charcoal. When the meres and marshes of the Great Fen were drained in the nineteenth century, the writer Charles Kingsley was able to articulate the sadness of their passing, while understanding and approving of the reasons why they had to go. 'A certain sadness is pardonable,' he wrote, 'to one who watches the destruction of a grand natural phenomenon, even though its destruction brings blessings to the human race.' He catalogued the loss, species by species, the patches of primeval forest and miles of reeds, the coot that clanked and the bittern that boomed, the hawks and kites, the ruffs and spoonbills and avocets and snipe, right down to the great copper butterfly and the insects of the fen: 'Ah, well, at least we shall have wheat and mutton instead, and no more typhus and ague.' Over time, we got what we wanted, and in the process we lost what we had.

The devastation was unrelenting, and continued well into our own age. Agricultural intensification following the Second World War further denuded what was left of our woods and heathland and meres. In the newly formed edgelands left behind after industry retreated, woods were once again able to begin the long process of re-establishing themselves in the spaces created, although nothing like to the degree of the post-glacial period, because of the much smaller time frame involved, and complicated by the fact of widespread human agency and development. But these derelict landscapes left largely to themselves are also exactly the kinds of places where new community forests are being constructed.

These are our postmodern woodlands, a man-made greening of wasteland and former industrial sites that has been going on over the past twenty years. You can easily get lost in the woods of mission statements and manifestos where community forests are concerned: the twelve woodlands established so far aim to 'deliver a comprehensive package of urban, economic and social regeneration', and are in the process of 'creating high-quality environments for millions of people by revitalising derelict land, providing new opportunities for leisure, recreation and cultural activities, enhancing biodiversity, preparing for climate change and supporting education, healthy living and social and economic development'.

These new woods are like green engines, designed to revive and regenerate. We haven't time to let our waste ground and mineral workings and backfields recreate their own environments, to find their own points of balance – even though our edgelands are already providing some of the most biodiverse habitats to be found in the country. Some of these young ecosystems, finding their footholds in our abandoned edgelands, are even cleared away and destroyed to make way for the new 'high-quality environments'. It feels like a green version of what happened in our inner cities after the war, when communities were cleared and moved on to outlying housing developments. Regeneration is such a seductive and powerful metaphor.

*

One of the most striking metaphors to arise from the (relatively) new science of genomics is 'progressive detachment'. This is part of an attempt to answer an apparently puzzling question. Why don't the most sophisticated forms of life have the most sophisticated genomes? Why should it be that a chimpanzee genome is simpler and shorter than a salamander's, and the human genome is simpler and shorter than a chimpanzee's?

The idea of 'progressive detachment' is that – throughout evolutionary history – genetic faults or errors have 'switched off' small parts of our genome. Gradually, we have had to adjust and compensate for the lack of these parts. If a blackbird's genome dictates that at the first sign of spring it must make a cup-shaped nest lined with mud and grass, then that's what it will do. Once that part of the genome is inactive, an animal is simultaneously blessed and cursed. If you lose the deep, instinctive pull to make a certain kind of shelter in a certain place at a certain time, then you can, in theory, make whatever kind of shelter you can think of, from an igloo to a skyscraper.

But if the blessing of 'progressive detachment' is liberation from instinctive behaviour, and from that comes the birth of civilisation, then the curse is a sense of loss and longing. If we were once creatures whose lives were mapped and printed on the earth by a set of deep instincts, then is it any wonder we wax lyrical about the hills, forests, rivers, moors? Does this explain our culture's recurring dream of going feral, back to nature, like the boys in *Brendon Chase*, reconnecting with our ancient lost instincts?

If nothing else, 'progressive detachment' is a beautiful, poetic idea. Science – especially a fast-moving new science like genomics – is a constantly shifting field of metaphors. The science itself changes, as new discoveries are made and new theories are advanced. But the metaphors change too, in an attempt to be more faithful to the evidence. Whatever happens to 'progressive detachment' as a theory of genomics, it will still remain a haunting and plausible story about our human past, and our connection with the environment.

*

If 'progressive detachment' hadn't emerged from genetic science, it would have been necessary for wilderness writers to invent it.

Whole books are spent trying to explain this pull, this yearning, this sense of a lost but essential connection to the earth. The Welsh have a word that comes close, but with a different twist. Welsh poets use the word '*hiraeth*', which describes an anguished sense of separation from home ground, from the land you know and love. It is much deeper than 'homesickness', but it is a kind of sickness. And the only cure, we're told, is to go back. Back home, back to the forests and mountains, press your nose to the ground and know that this is where you came from.

But there is an undertow to our yearning for wilderness that feels less comfortable. When you get to your wild place, who will you meet there? Whose hospitality will you call upon? Well, usually no one's, because the point of much wilderness writing, it seems, is to celebrate a yearning not just for wild places, but for wild places without any people in them. Is there a misanthropic edge to our national passion for wilderness writing and wilderness travel?

We would like to start a counter-movement. Rather than escaping to the forests of the Highlands, park your car at Matalan and have a walk around the edgelands woods. This has the added advantage that you won't die of exposure if you take a wrong turn. And if we must visit mountains, let's make sure there's always a café near the summit, so we can have a drink and enjoy the company of our fellow travellers. Snowdon has already taken this bold step. Now all we need is a Premier Inn on the top of Ben Nevis and a Little Chef on Scafell Pike. Let the campaign begin.

*

One of our rarest trees seems happiest shying away at the edge of the woods, even preferring open and high ground to thick forest. The whitebeam is one of the thirty-three trees native to Britain (those species that established a foothold early on in the present interglacial period, once the ice began to loosen its grip some 10,000 years ago), though it has an increasingly complicated taxonomy. There are actually many species of this tree, often endemic to particular areas, where they might be counted in the dozens or even fewer. We visit an example of the Lancaster whitebeam, *Sorbus lancastriensis*, near the village of Silverdale, on the edge of Morecambe Bay. To our untrained eyes, it looks like a whitebeam – it has that giveaway downy white underside to every leaf that lets the wind wink and shimmer through the tree – though expert eyes could tell the difference written into each of those leaves, their subtle variations in shape and pattern that distinguish this species from other whitebeams. This tree is one of only a couple of thousand, all of which are to be found in this northernmost corner of the old county of Lancashire.

Recent advances in DNA sampling mean that even greater genetic variation has been identified in whitebeams, and new species are being identified all the time. Wales and the West Country are particularly rich. Stirton's whitebeam, *Sorbus stirtoniana*, occurs only on the cliffs of Craig Breidden in Montgomeryshire, while the Llangollen whitebeam, *Sorbus cuneifolia*, is restricted to the cliffs of Eglwyseg Mountain in Denbighshire. At Methyr Tydfil, the Motley's whitebeam, *Sorbus motleyi*, is thought to be a hybrid of the Ley's whitebeam and rowan, probably crossed during the storm winds of 1989, when conditions for hybridisation to form were favourable: gaps and breaks in canopy cover allowed in enough new light for wind-dispersed seeds to germinate. Only two young trees are known to exist, both at one site.

There's something Ovidian about the way whitebeams assume the names of their finders, or locality; as if the trees are able to transmute language and place into their identity. A whitebeam standing at a lay-by near Watersmeet in Devon was for a long time suspected of being variant, and recently it was finally identified as one of a distinct species. Casting around for a name for this new kind of tree, botanists decided to reference the NO PARKING sign that had been nailed to its trunk for many years: and so the No Parking Whitebeam, Sorbus admonitor, came into being. These new whitebeams might offer a small reversal of our sense of the vanished forest. They continue to evolve and abide, and seem all the more vital for these graftings from the world of humans.

*

Edgelands woodlands are feral because most of them used to be tame. Some began life as gardens for long-demolished houses in what used to be the countryside before the cities grew. Others were copses left standing when those around were felled to make way for a factory or mill. On the southern edge of the Greater Manchester conurbation, where land was cleared to build Manchester Ringway Airport (initially as an RAF base in 1938), clumps of trees remain outside the perimeter of the airport, trees that once marked the corners of fields or farmyards. When plans were announced sixty years later for a second runway to be built, protesters took to these feral woodlands south of the airport as a protest. Why did they live in trees? Partly as a symbol of the wood-lands habitats they were seeking to protect, but largely because it made them harder to shift.

In recent years edgelands woodlands have been the scene of many a protest against development – new buildings, new roads, new runways. For those who climb in them, defend them, use them as defensible fortresses, these woods represent a bulwark against the encroachment of the urban on the rural. This is what the edgelands represent, a no-man's-land between the two sides, a touchstone on the constantly shifting border.

*

If edgelands woodlands and the new community woodlands do continue to spread their canopy over the landscape nearer to our cities, might we see a revival of deer hunting and coursing? In Scotland, this is already happening. In Glasgow, Dundee and Aberdeen, police have begun to report on a rise in urban hunting. Gangs armed with guns and crossbows, or using lurcher dogs, are stalking deer for the thrill of the chase, turning our community woods into the forest of anti-quity. The great difference of course is that the old forest was the preserve of the king or lord, supported by a hierarchy of subordinate hunting roles. But we are all lords of the manor now.

A hunt in the postmodern forest might begin with the weapons being inspected and made ready, the dogs quietened in their car cages. Next, a few lines of grey cocaine are chopped out with a supermarket loyalty card on the back of a CD case, and, suitably emboldened and excited, the caravan of 4 x 4s switches to full beam and enters the scratchy woodland. Leaving the vehicles at the car park, the party then moves ahead on foot, quietly through a dark scented with honeysuckle, wild rose and nightshade, over stiles and along footpaths, deeper into the woods, until the shout goes out and the dogs are let loose. The whole thing is recorded on cameraphones.

*

As schoolboys in industrial north-west England, we had our own very different versions of Brendon Chase, where housing estates opened on to building sites, railway sidings, scrublands. These were places we would play, for whole, long days, on bikes or with toy guns. But although our sense of adventure may have been the same as the Hensman brothers, their success in surviving for almost a year alone in the woods was determined by their knowledge of the natural world, their skill with shotguns and knives, their resourcefulness in shelter-building, fire-making, fishing.

As edgelands comprehensive schoolchildren in the Seventies, with our plastic guns and Chopper bikes, we wouldn't have lasted a weekend in our feral woodlands.

*

We stroll through an edgelands copse in the edgelands of Shrewsbury at dusk, listening to the traffic taper to a background hum, and watching the autumn leaves catch fire in the late sun. We are about to go home when we come across a strange happening. A TV crew is filming a man on horseback, dressed in full jousting garb. There is no one else in costume here, just a bored and cold gaggle of production assistants and runners taking notes and sipping coffee. The camera is on a track, and the movement of camera and horse keeps slipping out of sync, again and again. They run the camera back on its dolly, and try the shot again. The horse is snorting. The director is nervous, urging everyone to hurry up, to get it right this time. Are these edgelands playing Sherwood Forest, or Chrétien de Troyes' Arthurian French woodlands? Either way, the sun is fading fast, and the shot is not in the can.

Venues

We are told by psychologists that money spent on experiences contributes more to our happiness than money spent on things. You may argue that it depends what the 'things' are, and that some 'things' are so extraordinary that owning them becomes an experience in itself. A beautiful house overlooking the ocean, or (why hold back here?) your own private island complete with limpid warm lagoons, white-sand beaches and your own staff might constitute an experience, and might well contribute to your happiness. But let's not quibble. Money spent on a wonderful event or activity does feel like an investment. And where is the best place to seek out these ultimate experiences?

*

Apart from the leisure and entertainment multiplexes dotted across our edgelands, many of our key venues for sport, music, expos and even religious worship are to be found here. Football stadiums used to be close to the heart of the cities they served, and many of the oldest club grounds still are. Take Wolverhampton Wanderers, for example. Wolves have played their football at Molineux since 1889. Their stadium wasn't always painted orange and black like the team's shirts, and it didn't always have a large Asda superstore nestling in its shadow, but it has always been no more than a Derek Dougan volley away from the city centre. Elsewhere, though, as clubs have become more successful, and the fan base grows along with the TV revenues, some have found they need a new start in the edgelands.

When those other Wanderers – Bolton – set their hearts on a new stadium in the Nineties, the old Burnden Park ground, home to the club for a century, was abandoned. Their new home, the Reebok, was built on the Middlebrook Retail Park in Horwich, in the edgelands of Bolton, much to the frustration of many fans. But there is something fitting here.

*

The vestiges of popular religious behaviour survive in the heightened experience and spectacle of live sport and live music. Since Bill Shankly famously elevated football to the status of a religion ('Some say football's a matter of life and death, but I assure you it's much more serious than that') the comparison has become commonplace. And football in the edgelands has many of the properties of pilgrimage: a withdrawal from the place where you spend your days, a journey with others sharing a common purpose, a gathering in one place, a powerful sense of identity and belonging, an act of witnessing, a sense of participation.

*

There are few places as mysterious as a vast empty venue. In our edgelands journeys we have walked around the echoing lobbies and halls of the National Exhibition Centre near Birmingham out of season, looking at the posters for last year's and next year's bands. We have walked around the perimeter of an empty football stadium on a bright spring midweek afternoon. The huge car parks and service roads around the ground were clear, barring the odd car ferrying staff to and from the ground, and the odd wide-eyed visitor like us. The stadium – capable of so much sound and light and spectacle – in this switched-off state seemed as remote as a megalithic temple. Mind you, the football played by this unnamed team is a bit megalithic, too, in the view of these Old Trafford and Anfield pilgrims.

*

If edgelands venues have inbuilt pilgrimage potential, then perhaps it's no surprise to see a pattern from American religious culture beginning to emerge here – the out-of-town church. Where are the edgelands cathedrals? To find them, you must look to the groups, often young and unaffiliated to the mainstream denominations, that meet in the conference centres and leisure centres of the edgelands, because they cannot find a venue in the city large enough (or affordable enough) to hold their growing crowds of worshippers. These groups – often charismatic evangelicals in theology and practice – make a weekly pilgrimage out of the towns on the empty Sunday edgelands roads. Here, in a Victorian mill awaiting redevelopment, or in a sports hall or a warehouse, they can sing and pray as long and as loud as they want and be unheard by anyone except God and each other.

Mines

Writing for American *Vogue* in 1954, the poet W. H. Auden came up with what may be the first practical edgelands itinerary. In 'England: Six Unexpected Days', the poet suggested a driving tour of England for the adventurous American visitor. His proposed route managed to bypass the traditional scenic destinations and historic sites, taking the traveller north from Heathrow, through Ashby-de-la-Zouch and Crewe Junction (where Auden's idea of The North begins) up to Appletreewick. At this point the trail does enter the Yorkshire Dales National Park, created the same year Auden's tour was published (and allows room for a detour to Hawes in Wensleydale, whose cheese, we're told, a Mr Eliot is very fond of), then continues onwards to Keld at the head of Swaledale, then Dufton on the edge of the Eden Valley, before entering the high north Pennines, and the lead-mining country around Nenthead, Rookhope and Alston Moor.

Auden was perfectly at home in these edgelands: 'Tramlines and slagheaps, pieces of machinery, / That was, and still is, my ideal scenery,' he wrote in his *Letter to Lord Byron* in 1936. As a child, Auden had been obsessed with lead mining, living in an imaginary universe of slag heaps, washing floors and winding gear. He constructed his own private world ('the basic elements of which were a landscape, northern and limestone, and an industry, lead mining') largely out of books: early reading included *Machinery for Metalliferous Mines* and *Lead and Zinc Ores of Northumberland and Alston Moor*. He outgrew the obsession, but a fascination, even a deep reverence, for this abandoned mining landscape never quite deserted his imagination, and is a recurring theme throughout his writing life, a deep aquifer he returned to.

On a drizzly and short January day we visit Rookhope, the north Pennine village where, in *New Year Letter*, Auden described dropping pebbles into a mineshaft, and 'heard / the reservoir of darkness stirred'. We're as far as it's possible to be in northern England from city or conurbation, and yet the landscape here does have an unkempt, edgelands quality. Derelict mine buildings, function unknown, stand forgotten in woodland along the burn; old tracks and washing floors scar the moorland, and there are more recent remains: rusting winding gear, huts of stone and tin, scarred areas littered with oil drums and pieces of machinery. The rain begins siling it down. The high moor hereabouts is probably the most austere and sombre terrain we've walked through.

What was it Auden found here? Some dark, mineral implacability to set against the Romantic Lakes far to the west? A negative epiphany of 'Self and Not-self, Death and Dread'? Did the time he spent building those imaginary childhood mines prepare him for the making of poems, a real pebble dropped into an actual shaft marking the borderline between the safety of the childhood world and the estrangement of the adult? The wreckage of lead mining lies about the valley, reclaimed and redeveloped only by nature, unlike its landscaped lowland carboniferous counterparts. But searching these abandoned mines for clues feels like combing the moorland grasses and heather of a watershed for the single pristine source of a river.

*

John Barr's *Derelict Britain*, published in 1969, paints a grim picture. The defacement and degradation the county had arrived at (with the Seventies just around the corner – if only they knew) was largely the result of a long tolerance of an unquestioned equation: muck = money. Waterways had long been abandoned, railways were still reeling from Dr Beeching's severe rationalisation measures, industrial junklands and forsaken military lands blighted the landscape. The overwhelming despoliation, however, seems to have been brought about by mining of one sort or another. Collieries and their slag heaps and slurry ponds, China clay workings, old quarries, gravel pits, 'all the extractive industries, essential for national prosperity, yet which gouge and tear the earth to bring out well over 400 million tons of useable minerals every year, the waste too often hurled about with no more conscience than a toddler shows towards his just-smashed toys'.

Of course, the little we knew of it, as young children growing up in Lancashire at that time, seemed like paradise. That landscape of heaps and holes is less evident now, and many of us even live surprisingly close to mining's former sites and spaces, reclaimed and landscaped. But our edgelands are still full of its scars and traces. The exhilarating ugliness that J. B. Priestley found almost bracing between Manchester and Bolton in the Thirties is still easily detectable. From the train, the land lies hilly in places and sombre; stands of new trees and scubby woodland break to reveal mounds of earth, or pools of dark water.

We start a walk at Lumn's Lane, roughly equidistant from Manchester and Bolton, in Pendlebury, partly because of Priestley, partly because we like the name on the map, and partly because we know the painter L. S. Lowry lived and worked in this area. Metal railings, buddleia, abandoned pieces of furniture, a silted canal and implausible footpaths: classic edgelands. Pendlebury was a coal-producing area since the early years of the Industrial Revolution, a place of collieries and mills. The pits have gone, but the land itself has been altered by their activity, and gives off an air of menace. We don't recommend visiting this area alone. Under a low grey sky, even the foliage seems angrily lit from within. It's the kind of place where cars might be abandoned, where things could be quietly dumped in the roadside overgrowth, where you find yourself checking your phone for signal strength. Eventually, we climb to the top of the old landfill site, and a view down the Irwell Valley towards the city of Manchester opens up. It isn't ugly at all, really, but the ground underfoot is shaley, friable, a dead giveaway that this is old mining land.

*

We think what excited us about mines as children was the huge hidden depths they suggested. Beneath our back fields and roads, far below the ordinary and the humdrum, there were deep mineral galleries. Even the most modest colliery – scaling down or decommissioned by the time we were growing up – might have sunk shafts that radiated propped passages for miles beneath us. Mining adjusted your sense of time, the coal measures a submerged forest that had lived in an impossible, geological prehistory. Long thought over, this imponderable that lay beneath us worked on and altered our sense of ourselves in time. We began to conceive of larger spaces around us in terms of seams and layers, and of our lifetime's span – the half-hour buses to town, school, the train to the coast, Saturday-night television and being allowed to stay up one hour later in the holidays, the roof tar melted in summer and the water mains frozen in winter, everything, and all that was to come –

reduced to a rusty sliver in the earth. It put us in our place. Mining was deeper and more profound than even the grave. As the poet Tony Harrison was to observe in his poem V after visiting his parents' plot on Beeston Hill above Leeds, the dead themselves might be undermined, collapsing into the void of a worked-out pit.

*

Auden became an international poet in motion, a bird of passage spending summers in Europe and wintering in the United States. He carried his 'significant earth' with him wherever he went, as well as an OS map of Alston Moor, which he fixed to the walls of his shack on Fire Island or the house he bought at Kirchstetten.

Norman Nicholson and Jack Clemo, on the other hand, were residents. Almost exact contemporaries (both born during the First World War) they were poets of two different kinds of mining land-scape, each at opposite ends of England, and they both lived their whole lives rooted within their own small communities.

Nicholson's place was Millom in Cumberland. He grew up on the edge of the Lake District, but studiously avoided its interior land-scape, the echo chamber of English Romanticism. Instead, Nicholson was a poet of the west coast, of Whitehaven and Cleator Moor and Egremont, the west Cumberland scarred by the 'iron rush' for haematite ore and coal mining. Even in his earliest work, human industry is set against slow diurnal and natural forces: curlews in an estuary where bombing practice is taking place; pit heaps that 'build barriers against the light'; a river that runs 'red as rhubarb' stained with iron ore; pylons sprouting on the fells. Throughout his life, his place remained the same, but the focus deepened, and by the later poems Nicholson was able to draw on all of the forces of family and community living on this border country between

Romantic and industrial. Much of the industrial landscape he was born into went into decline during his lifetime, but he was alert to its vitality and longevity. He addressed Wordsworth's River Duddon sonnet sequence, and the lines: 'Child of the clouds! remote from every taint / Of sordid industry thy lot is cast':

> I laughed once at those words – for there, near where he
>   pondered
> On Duddon Bridge, shallow-draft barges shot their ore,
> Even in Wordsworth's day, for the charcoal-burning furnace
> Sited like a badger's sett deep in Duddon woods.

In this poem, 'On the Dismantling of Millom Ironworks', there's a Wordsworthian echo of 'the form remains: the function never dies', as the river rediscovers its former course and channels after many decades of haematite extraction, and the wind 'resumes its Right of Way'. Something like a natural balance is restored. But the poem is more complicated than that. As they dismantle the ironworks, the poet recognises how they have also 'shovelled my childhood / on to a rubbish heap'. There's a sense of a way of life being dismantled, too, of the generations being superannuated with an unrestricted, smokeless view of a river flowing 'untainted now, to a bleak, depopulated shore'.

*

Jack Clemo was born poor in the clay-land village of Goonamarris, and lived for decades in the hamlet of St Stephen's, blind for much of his adult life and deaf from his forties onwards. Growing up in a four-roomed granite cottage, the clay works where his father had been employed as a kiln worker were the landscape of his childhood, strange and alienating, a brutal disruption to the natural cycles. He was an evangelical Christian, a Nonconformist with roots in Calvinism. But for Clemo, the clay pools and spoil heaps and gouged earth became a mystical landscape. His early poems are littered with the waste and debris of clay mining, and in its dereliction he finds a sounding board for his own bleak visions: 'I saw tip-waggons bombard earth's beauty/ Until my faith caught their mood.' He was beginning to suffer the first isolating bouts of his blindness and deafness, and his poems spoke with an astringency that gave short shrift to Romantic ideas of nature, or even love. The speaker in 'The Clay-Tip Worker', which begins like one of John Clare's lyrical hymns, seems to take pleasure in the effects his business is having on the natural world:

> I love to see the sand I tip
> Muzzle the grass and burst the daisy heads.
> I watch the hard waves lapping out to still
> The soil's rhythm for ever, and I thrill
> With solitary song upon my lip,
> Exulting as the refuse spreads:
> 'Praise god, the earth is maimed,
> And there will be no daisies in that field
> Next spring; it will not yield
> A single bloom or grass blade: I shall see
> In symbol potently
> Christ's Kingdom there restored:
> One patch of Poetry reclaimed
> By Dogma: one more triumph for our Lord.'

For decades before he met his wife, Ruth, in his fifties, Clemo's faith gave him a conviction that he was 'elect for marriage'. His love for his wife, and a subsequent deepening of his faith, changed the character of his work. His poems continued to excavate and draw upon the world of the claypit, but now the clay was light, sensual, the raw material of 'the patterned cup for the great Marriage-feast'. The lunar landscape of clay mining itself gradually became the setting for visionary poems of salvation and redemption. Unlike Nicholson's, Clemo's industrial landscape outlasted him, as demand for kaolin increased with its seemingly endless utility. Eleven years after his death in 1994, his cottage at St Stephen's was demolished by the Goonvean China Clay Co. He would, surely, have been fascinated by the moonbase climate domes of the Eden Project, built in a kaolin pit just a few miles away that has been redeemed from the white landscape.

*

In later life, Auden described his face as 'a wedding cake left out in the rain'. (Sitting for David Hockney, the artist is reported to have wondered: 'I kept thinking, if his face looks like this, what must his balls look like.') It was a face fissured and cracked, geological even, and it's easy to draw comparisons with limestone landscapes. Auden might have eroded with age to resemble his landscape of the mind, but his connection to it, however profound, was always imaginative; the miners who worked the dwindling lead deposits and the people who lived in mining communities remained, as he wrote in a later poem, 'nameless to me / faceless as heather or grouse'.

In December 1972 Auden was in Newcastle-upon-Tyne for a reading, where a lunch party arranged to drive the poet out to Roman Wall country, and the edges of the lead-mining region. Auden shuffled down in his carpet slippers, and shook no hands.

The group included Sid Chaplin, a former Wearside miner, who had started out writing between shifts and eventually published novels and short stories, but his introduction to Auden got things off to a bad start. On being told Chaplin also wrote, Auden replied: 'Oh, I see, a regional writer.' The party drove out to a pub at Chollerford, Auden chain-smoking his Senior Service, and according to Chaplin's notes, rallying briefly once they got talking of mining:

A spark of life only when I got the drinks in The George (his a dry Martini on the rocks), when he discovered that I'd been a miner Bishop Auckland way. Momentarily his eyes lit up. He talked of Rookhope, still lead mining when he knew it. When did he first go? At 12. His father a doctor interested in geology, his brother in Geological Survey. His two most treasured books, he told me, the *Geological Survey of Weardale* (1923) and Westgarth Foster's *Sections of the Strata from Newcastle upon Tyne to Alston*. Said I was the first person he'd met who had read the latter. My note: 'Obviously little or no feeling for folk – I doubt if he'd ever made friends with a Weardale or Alston lead miner'. Quoted Chesterton and Karl Kraus.

Miners themselves had already articulated and described their own working lives and environments; writers like Chaplin or artists such as Norman Cornish at the Spennymoor Settlement, or Oliver Kilbourn and the Ashington Group of painters (a story since dramatised by Lee Hall in *The Pitmen Painters* in 2008), a school of artists that had formed in 1934, who found themselves applauded by the London art establishment. In between shifts at Woodhorn and Ellington pits, the men had begun to attend art appreciation classes at Ashington YMCA, supported by a lecturer supplied by the Workers' Educational Association. They painted their environment, life in the pit village communities, allotments and pigeon crees, the dog track and the corner shop, working with bulk-bought Walpamur paint and using boards and plywood which they prepared with whiting or size.

The war disrupted the Ashington Group, but they carried on, out of sight of metropolitan attention now, meeting and working in a hut at the end of a cinder track just past the Ashington Co-op. The art critic William Feaver visited them there in 1971, and found himself sitting by a fire in a storeroom shack full of decades of art. The hut was demolished the year before the miners' strike and the dismantling of the coal industry itself. Some of the north-east colliery fields, like Seaham, have managed to survive the decades since by attracting new industry, building industrial estates and even establishing an expensive hotel and 'serenity spa' at Seaham Hall (where Lord Byron lived for a while); others, like Easington (the setting for another of Hall's dramas, Billy Elliot), have collapsed completely. The literature and art that happened here makes us wonder about all of the other working communities that never found a way of expressing and recording their lives and environments, which have passed from the face of the earth leaving only scars and traces. The Ashington and Spennymoor artists turned an edge into a centre, taking matters of representation into their own hands, as Sid Chaplin described:

The living are caught before they go; the pigeon fanciers, corner-enders, offshift miners squatting on their hunkers and soaking in the sunshine and the good crack. In a moment the bus will come and the buzzer blow for the backshift. Now it is all recorded, time cannot take away the seven ages of man and woman – his grandmother, mother, sisters, wife and daughter; or his father and brothers, his friends and pit marras. Soon the baby will be a small boy: he will change: a drawing or painting is a shot against time.

Power

There are no signposts leading to the edgelands, no motorway signs with speed-legible Transport font and preordained background colour pointing us towards their fastnesses. Edgelands aren't *sites*. They don't behave like castles or bird reserves or historic market towns. Nobody asks, *Are we there yet?*

But there are other kinds of signs, and none truer or more emphatic than the sight of cooling towers in the distance. Looming grey elephantine hulks, they designate the in-betweenness of the landscape you are passing through. Inland cooling towers declare our coal-fired stations. They are part of the edgelands, but in a sense atypical of them; in the great interfacial zones, so much goes unnoticed, but a power station is difficult to miss or even to take for granted as part of a familiar journey.

*

We know now that language acts upon us, rather than functioning simply as one of our actions. The work of philologists like Lakoff and Johnson has uncovered the extent of the super-saturation of our language with metaphors, and psychologists have shown us how these metaphors unconsciously change our understanding of ourselves and the world around us.

These insights have been turned into popular currency by the self-help industry, so airport bookstalls now offer you the chance to 're-programme your mind for success', 'unleash the tiger within', and use techniques like 'neuro-linguistic programming' to change your life for the better. If – as researchers have claimed – we are so sensitive to metaphor that students sitting on 'hard' chairs are overwhelmingly more likely to describe their exam paper as 'hard', then the edgelands could be the next big thing in personal development.

Imagine, if you will, a group of stressed-out executives being bussed out to what they regard as the middle of nowhere. They are herded off the bus, and urged to stand in a ring, holding hands around what looks like a giant concrete elephant's foot. Now feel the force of the metaphors. The metaphors here could hardly be bettered. Stand in the shadow of the 'cooling towers'. Watch your anxieties turn to wisps of smoke and twist into the ether. Feel your pent-up frustrations drawn out of you by this irresistible updraught. You are 'cooling', but you will not leave here empty. You are in a 'power station'. Feel the force. Every minute you spend here, you are more empowered. Feel that power building up inside you. Now you are the 'power station'.

From now on, you only have to glimpse a cooling tower to feel a rush of positive energy, a surge of voltage. Now make that call, take that risk, close that deal, seize that promotion.

*

For any of us who pass by a power station up close, such as those who regularly commute through Rugeley in Staffordshire aboard a Virgin West Coast train (where the links of the Lakeside Golf Club – good edgelands visible from every green – only seem to accentuate the scale and drama of the approach), or saw Tinsley in South Yorkshire from the M1 (before its towers were demolished in 2008), the looming effect can be dramatic and overwhelming. Cooling towers distort our sense of scale in the English landscape. They also introduce a new spectrum of available visible effects to this thing called the country-side. Seen on a cold dawn, they seem to shimmer over the frozen landscape, mirage-like; while the last late light of June catching their upper reaches 300 feet up can find in their grey concrete a warm range of pinks and purples like a mesa sunset.

So many of our power stations are only seen and known from a distance, concrete colossuses that loom and hold their relative position on the horizon as our car or train presses on through the landscape. The flat country where Lincolnshire, Nottinghamshire and Yorkshire meet is particularly blessed, and from the former liquorice fields around Pontefract it's possible to see three power stations in the distance.

Which is where many people prefer them. It might be better if they weren't visible at all. Power stations are brutal, dirty and ugly, eyesores spoiling the view, which use our ancient river systems as coolants, before releasing their ghosts into the air as plumes that stretch the length of counties.

Up close, though, a cooling tower's hyperboloid structure can be truly appreciated, and from its base the view up is strangely vertiginous, the wall drawing narrower before billowing outwards again near the apex. The block construction from concrete, flat-tened and disguised by distance, comes into sharper focus, and we begin to appreciate its vertical world of algae and mosses that have made it their home. Might the dark stain visible at the lip of towers be as reliable an indicator of true north as moss on a tree trunk in a Ray Mears fantasy of backwoods disorientation?

Silent from a distance, as you approach a cooling tower on foot, you're aware of a rising white noise, a watery roar. Looking up a tower's skirt is a revelation. The view inside is of hundreds of piers standing in a heavy downpour, so powerful you can barely see the daylight across on the opposite side. It looks like some vast, drenched film set; the industrial, warm, interior rain that falls in *Stalker* or *Blade Runner*.

Cooling towers also generate stories and myths. It could be their giant size and implacability, or it could be their connection with water. Humans have had a natural tendency to associate spirits with bodies of water since antiquity, and the Greeks knew of several species of naiads related to different kinds of fresh water to be found in their world: there were the Crinaease found at fountains, the Limnades or Limnatides who haunted lakes, the Pegaeae who dwelt in springs, the Potameides who watched over rivers, and the Eleionomae who occupied marshes and lured travellers astray like landlocked sirens.

If standing water – pools, lakes, bogs – were the liminal, sacred places of our northern pagan ancestors, then maybe these are ours: vast man-made water temples. The power station at Didcot has been called the Cathedral of the Vale, and it *was* designed by Frederick Gibberd, the architect who gave us Liverpool's Roman Catholic Cathedral (the concrete 'Paddy's Wigwam', as it is sometimes referred to in those parts). In one sense, all power stations are Cathedrals of the Electric Light Bulb and Kettle.

*

Cooling towers stand as deceptively still as mills once did, but are full of busy, watery activity. When a curious child on a train points and asks his father what a cooling tower is, and he replies, 'That's where they make the clouds,' the imagination is plumbed in again to an ancient sense of water spirits, the modern connected to the mythical and fabulous. There was a story in the Nineties concerning a poet who'd become obsessed with cooling towers, and who'd engaged himself in the composition of his magnum opus, a long and ambitious work conflating each of the nine Muses with a chimney. The trouble was, he couldn't find a power station which had nine cooling towers; some, such as those at Fiddlers Ferry, Ratcliffe-on-Soar and Ferrybridge came tantalisingly close, having eight apiece, while others either fell a few short (as at Rugely, with four, or Didcot, which has six) or were too generously appointed (as at Drax, where there are twelve, the biggest cluster in Europe). Left with only the schema, the bare conceptual bones of his great work – never the best way to approach the writing of a poem – he was deserted by the Muse, and is said to have never written again.

*

The silver suits and monorails we might have expected of the future have never materialised, but power stations are places where banks of big important dials and gauges have thrived, a Gerry Anderson film set made real. Inside every one, somebody keeps a constant vigil, checking the National Grid's vital obs, watching an unwavering, steady line of output, a region's energy pulse. Fluctuations in demand have to be met: the cliché of a hundred thousand kettles coming to the boil at once during a commercial break is accurate enough. At the centre of any power station, powerful reactors or furnaces have to be managed safely, a military exercise in constant surveillance and containment.

At Ratcliffe-on-Soar, the men on the afternoon shift have time to answer our questions. One has brought apples in his lunch box, picked from a garden in the next county, he tells us. It seems a relaxed, swivel-chair kind of a posting, though something in their work clothes – bright boiler suits, big boots – militates against too much of a sense of this being a desk job. The coal furnace here is fine, so long as it's treated with great respect, and is compared to 'a lion in its cage'. We're taken to see it. The air inside the turbine hall smells of hot metal, iron filings, and the gantries and walkways vibrate underfoot. A hatch is opened on to the furnace, where coal dust is being ignited: it's like being allowed a glimpse into the vent of a volcano, an oven gust from the innermost circle of an inferno, raging in the middle of Nottinghamshire.

*

Getting close on foot can be difficult, though some enlightened stations do organise regular guided tours. But if you want to take a virtual tour, you could always try Facebook: the Great Climate Swoop of autumn 2009 encouraged direct action and peaceful protest, together with useful photos of perimeter fences with captions like 'Not sure if there's a hole here?' Coal-fired power stations have become politically charged, part of the front line in an eco battleground, in a way that would have been difficult to imagine a couple of decades ago, when coal meant solidarity with the striking miners for many interested in protest and resistance. Now, as most of the UK's nuclear power stations have begun or completed a long process of decommissioning, and the urgency of accelerating climate change has formed a shift in public opinion and a significant movement of activists, burning fossil fuels is beyond the pale. Police and protesters are clashing outside coal-fired power stations; towers are being climbed by protesters equipped with food and supplies.

*

In the late Thirties, the modernist poet and artist David Jones, like other modernists before him, questioned whether it was still possible to discern the sacred, the transcendent, in the new technological forms and systems that were changing our landscape and culture. In his poem 'A, a, a, Domine Deus' Jones offers an account of this quest:

> I have looked for a long while
> > at the textures and contours.
> I have run a hand over the trivial intersections.
> I have journeyed among the dead forms
> causation projects from pillar to pylon.
> I have tired the eyes of the mind
> > regarding the colours and lights.
> I have felt for His Wounds
> > in nozzles and containers.
> I have wondered for the automatic devices.
> I have tested the inane patterns
> > without prejudice.
> I have been on my guard
> > not to condemn the unfamiliar.
> For it is easy to miss Him
> > at the turn of a civilisation.

For Jones, this quest to see 'the Living God projected from the Machine' was ultimately fruitless. The fault-line between past and technological present seemed like a chasm. But what would David Jones make of the edgelands, if he were still with us, and if we could coax him out of his one-room 'bunker' in Harrow, where he worked on his epic poems, watercolours and inscriptions?

Cooling towers are no longer simply a symbol of technological change. They are morally and politically complex and contentious.

For many, they are chilling symbols of ecological meltdown. For the English painter Roger Wagner the mixed message of the cooling towers was a direct inspiration for a number of paintings, but notably *Menorah* from 1993. The menorah is a seven-branched candlestick 'with cups made like almond-blossoms? . . . the whole of it one beaten work of pure gold'. In the biblical book of Exodus, Moses places the menorah in the Tabernacle in front of the Holy of Holies, where God dwells with his people. Said to symbolise the burning bush, the menorah has become one of Judaism's central symbols. Wagner explained the genesis of his painting:

When I first saw Didcot power station through the window of a train from Oxford to Paddington, the smoke belching from the central chimney reminded me more of a crematorium than a symbol of God's presence. And yet having said that, the astonishing sky behind the towers looked like the arch of some great cathedral, while something in the scale of the cooling towers themselves, with the light moving across them and the steam slowly, elegiacally, drifting away, created the impression that they were somehow the backdrop of a great religious drama. Both these ideas remained in my mind for many years, and developed in a series of paintings and sketches. On the one hand the crematorium-like chimney and the inhuman scale of the buildings brought associations with the industrial genocide of the twentieth century and the blank inhumanity of so much in human existence, while on the other hand within the strange beauty of the scene was the insistent sense of some great redemptive moment. It wasn't until I realised that the towers, from the angle I had seen them, had lined up to form the shape of the Menorah, that I realised how these two impressions could be united, and realised that the drama to which they were the backdrop must be the drama of the Crucifixion.

*

Are power stations a marker of edgelands? Are they a defining characteristic? They do bear one of the hallmarks of edgelands buildings – a function we can't live without, but don't want to live with. Whether it is sewage farms, car-crushers or power stations, edgelands are the place for these essential, invisible functions. We want them close enough to serve us, but far enough to be ignored.

But this subtle measure can change when a perceived danger – either from pollution or accident – enters the picture. Public fears can push some edgelands features out into rural territory. This was the fate of many great coal-fired power stations, and of nuclear power stations like Dungeness in Kent. Now, with wind farms cropping up on Cumbrian fells and gale-swept brows in the Scottish lowlands, we are at it again, pushing power generation out beyond our cities, beyond our edgelands, into what remains of the rural. And, of course, this brings protests, too, on grounds of aesthetics and noise pollution. This is what happens when the edgelands place a large boot-print into the countryside.

So let's bring power generation back where it belongs. Bring on the edgelands wind farms. How majestic it would be, on our way into or out of our cities, to drive past strips of giant white daffodils blowing in the breeze. Of course, some will say that there is insufficient wind in the lowlands on the edge of cities. But this is where the people come in. If we all agree to exhale when we step out of Carpet World . . .

*

England's edgelands are the next big thing in photography. After all, photographing gritty urban locations is now likely to lead to arrest on suspicion of planning a terrorist attack, and if you photograph rural Britain you are on very well-trodden ground.

This is not to say that edgelands are untouched by the lens. Far from it. Great photographers like William Eggleston and Bernd and Hilla Becher have built their careers on these overlooked landscapes. But their edgelands were in the southern states of America, or in Germany. Eggleston's notion of the 'democratic' function of photography, to step aside from received ideas of what is beautiful or romantic, has influenced a generation of art-school trained photographers. But it has sent most of them into the city.

Because the edgelands tend to have more freedom from the watchful eyes of city planners and residents worried about house prices, they can throw up shapes and forms that don't look quite like anywhere else. The Bechers' approach was perfectly suited to these landscapes. They were fascinated by the range and beauty of design in industrial buildings and landscapes, although that design process was driven by function rather than style. Like Victorian collectors with their cabinets of eggs or insects, this photographer couple collected and catalogued industrial buildings. In the early Seventies, their attention turned to cooling towers, and they printed the images like sheets from an inventory, nine or ten towers to a page. The effect of this repeated pattern was very powerful. A single cooling tower may look beautiful, but nine cooling towers on one sheet looks like a series of ancient monoliths, or temples, or plinths for statues of long-forgotten gods.

One of the most remarkable photographs of cooling towers is a black-and-white image of Agecroft power station (west of the Irwell near Pendlebury in Lancashire) made in 1983 by John Davies. In collections of his work such as *A Green and Pleasant Land* and *The British Landscape* (which includes 'Agecroft Power Station') Davies has proved himself to be a fascinated observer and recorder of industry and post-industry, of places where the pastoral and the urban coexist in our hinterlands. The four cooling towers recede in line on a plain, where pylons carry electricity away into the distance; the image is taken from higher ground, and suddenly the eye notices the tiny footballers, playing Sunday League matches on playing fields shadowed by the towers' steam; a few cars have gathered in the foreground, under the dark winter trees, where a white horse stands on fly-tipped ground. The overall effect is of life going on, anyhow, even in the shadow of the epic and monumental, and is as close as a photograph might have come to the 'untidy spot' of Auden's 'Musée des Beaux Arts': we almost expect the horse to rub its 'innocent behind' on one of those trees.

Go there now, to the ridge above the Irwell Valley (as we did in the previous chapter), and you'll find little of this remains. The towers were demolished in the Nineties (though the blasting was delayed for a pair of nesting peregrines). Many of the landscapes Davies photographed in the English lowlands are landscapes on the move. The cooling towers, once so new and strange, have already been redeveloped and are receding into the past.

Pallets

Pallets, like hi-vis smocks and supermarket trolleys, are invisible because of their ubiquity. They go out into the world and circulate, carrying goods into the centres of our cities, or emerge from the dark of sea containers with their loads hidden under opaque shrink-wrapping. The stronger hardwood varieties are hired, recycled, subject to no-deposit, no-return rules, though we might notice them then, when they are paused and idle in the edgelands, stacking into towers forty-high, rising even higher than shelterbelts of cypress and leylandii in business parks.

These are the clearing houses of consumerism. And also the de facto barometers of economic health. The quarterly GDP figures are reported, distant abstractions of gloom, but in the edgelands it's possible to look at the changing state of the pallet hire yards as to a pine cone: just as the latter's closing scales mean damp air is moving in, so the higher stacks speak of slowdown, inactivity, inertia.

Pallets are consumer capitalism's red blood cells. They convey the products around the organism. Unless you have taken this book to the top of a mountain to read (and we'd strongly discourage such frippery) then the chances are you're surrounded by things from places far away, borne here on a pallet. And even if you *are* in the middle of nowhere, look to the labels on your clothes and wonder at the distances they've travelled. Pallets move the goods around. If we isolate the pallet, as Stephen Dedalus isolated the butcher boy's basket in Joyce's *A Portrait of the Artist as a Young Man*, pluck it out from the slur and texture of the everyday and consider it, self-contained, against the background of space, the thing it most resembles is a magic carpet with rigor mortis.

*

We decide to visit a pallet yard in Birmingham's edgelands. It is a large and busy place, with a steady stream of lorries sweeping in for reloading. Pleasing to the eye, all the pallets are blue, stacked as high as the buildings that surround the yard. It's a powder blue, like the blue-painted decking of seaside-themed cafés and shops. In the late-summer sun it looks like a Lego city. Children would love this place, climbing up the walls and tottering across the roofs. But, of course, no play is permitted. Health-and-safety notices are prominent on the outside and inside of the buildings. Hard hats, lorries, forklift trucks, hi-vis jackets, no unauthorised personnel in the pallet yard.

We head into what looks like the main building. The door is open. There is no one around. We follow a long corridor round the outside of the building, which leads to an office with a glass screen. This must be where the drivers come to have their order papers authorised. We wait, until a young woman arrives at the desk. She knows most of the people who come to her threshold, but she doesn't know us.

'A book?'

'Yes, a book about the edgelands.'

'The what?'

'Pallets. It's about pallets.'

'What do you want to do?'

'Look at the pallets in the yard.'

'Just look at them?'

'Well, photograph them and write about them.'

'I can't let you take photographs.'

'Why not?'

'I can't authorise that. You'll have to speak to head office if you want to do that.'

'We'll just write about them, then.'

'What d'you mean?'

'We'll just look at them and write about them.'

'Will you need to sit down?'

'No, we can write standing up, thank you.'

★

Pallets should be tagged, so their stories can be told. How many warehouses in how many countries? What trials of strength and endurance in the Southern Ocean on vast container ships? If the British public will turn out for a pencil museum, or a hat museum – and they do – then World of Pallets must be in with a chance. When the bottom falls out of the British haulage business, the pallet yards could be turned into play centres outside and museums inside.

Until recently, we, the consumers, were kept from the pallets that serve us. Unless you worked in a warehouse, or for a haulage firm (sorry, a logistics firm), or drove a forklift truck, you only saw the products on the shop shelves, cut free from the pallets that sandwiched them from factory to shop. Now, in the race to cut costs and snare customers, more and more edgelands-based mega-stores are letting you pick your products fresh from the pallets, and flogging them cheaper as a result. Here, warehouse and shop are one, and forklift trucks haunt the same aisles as the shoppers. Catering packs of rice or firkin-sized coffee tins are offered to us as a way of saving money. But that's not their only appeal. We live in an apocalyptic age, and although the scenarios shift on the TV news – bird flu, swine flu, financial meltdown, terrorism, rogue states, global warming – many British households are subtly stocking up, just in case. After all, being locked in your own cellar for months is a grim enough prospect, but at least you should have a stash of tea bags.

*

Pallets are the customary fuel for public bonfires now. We mean, of course, wooden pallets, the classic pallet. None of your plastic or metal nonsense here, just the classic cross-hatch, flatbed, wooden pallet. We are not fussy about colours. Powder blue is nice, but we appreciate that the colour often denotes a particular cargo or weight limit. And besides, you cannot see the colour for long once the flames take hold.

Across the country, early November sees the first big fire of the winter, accompanied by rockets, Catherine wheels, Roman candles. Families gather on the local cricket field, football pitch, pub car park or village green to drink warm cans of beer and test out (on this one night of the year) the 'firework' setting on their digital camera.

These roaring, mountainous public bonfires are astonishing even for adults, but for children, feeling the sting on their faces hundreds of yards away, they hold a magical terror, and leave a lasting memory. In a passage from his remarkable sequence of poems 'Mercian Hymns', Geoffrey Hill recalls a childhood bonfire:

> We gaped at the car-park of 'The Stag's Head' where a bonfire
> of beer-crates and holly-boughs whistled above the new tar.

And the chef stood there, a king in his new risen hat, sealing
his brisk largesse with 'any mustard?'.

This is Hill's Mercia, the vast and growing edgelands of the West
Midlands. Now, 'Mercia' is more familiar as a police force than a
stretch of ancient land. The Stag's Head of Hill's boyhood has likely
been superseded by a newly built pub-cum-eaterie, with a
Travelodge attached, handily located on the intersection of three
major roads. And the beer crates that fuelled his childhood bonfire
will be pallets now, although pallets – as health and safety will
remind us – should not be lit lightly. Many are treated with pesticides, fungicides, preservatives. These pallets do so much foreign
travel that they have to convince border authorities that they cannot
harbour stowaways – diseases or parasites.

What became of the kegs and barrels, the tea chests of yester-
year, before the dawning of the age of the pallet? Were they all burnt
at charity bonfires? No doubt some were. Others still rot in corners
of the edgelands. And some are reborn as tables for theme pubs
or props for post-industrial shopping malls. Where are the coopers
now? Do their genes carry a blueprint for the making of barrels,
ready to be utilised when we tire of pallets? We won't hold our
breath. Instead, we await the emergence of a new British surname
– Palleteer, or Palletan.

*

Our visit to the Mercian pallet yards coincides with the earliest
rumblings of an election campaign. We didn't know it at the time,
but this was to be one of the longest, ugliest and emptiest election
campaigns Britain had ever seen. It was also to be played out so
fully in the media that it would seem as 'virtual' as Emmerdale or

Holby City. Unless we see them with our own eyes, how can we know that 'Gordon Brown', 'David Cameron' or 'Nick Clegg' are based on real people? Even if we met them face to face, they may still be method actors, staying in role, offering the public an 'immersive experience' in the drama called 'Who will govern us?'.

The night after the pallet-yard visit, the ten o'clock TV news shows footage of David Cameron on the hustings somewhere in the heart of England. But for edgelands enthusiasts the wide-shots are more arresting than the close-ups. All the while that the leader of the opposition is seen debating with good townspeople of wherever, he is standing on a pallet. And it isn't just any pallet. It is a powder-blue pallet. It could have been one of the pallets we saw earlier in the day. Now this is news.

We text each other. Look at that pallet! And who says there wouldn't be a market for a World of Pallets museum? All it would take is a bit of creative categorising: 'Pallets in Wartime', 'Pallets at Sea', 'How Pallets are Made', 'A Pallet for All Seasons', 'Pallets and Pests' and now 'Pallets in Politics'. Sounds like the start of a business plan.

*

Why does no one on *Desert Island Discs* ever ask for a stack of pallets as their luxury? Perhaps it wouldn't be allowed. It would be too useful. With the help of some nearby creepers, or strips of tree bark soaked and twisted into rope, a shelter could be fashioned. Or if you would rather not stay, why not lash some pallets into a handy raft? Those same local groups across the country that build giant pallet bonfires every winter often make pallet rafts in summer.

Charity raft races are a staple of bank holiday entertainment, wherever a river or harbour can be cleared for the purpose. The

Lego-like ability of pallets to become whatever building or vehicle you want them to be has made them perfect for such ventures. And this has led to a new branch of woodwork for hobbyists – 'Pallet Crafts'.

Among the main sources of inspiration for 'Pallet Crafts' is the American DIY magazine *ReadyMade*, and among their suggested pallet-based projects is a (yes, powder-blue) nautical-themed bedroom makeover, built around a bed on a platform made from old pallets. 'Pallet Crafts' are still in their infancy compared with – for example – matchstick modelling. For decades now, we have grown used to items in regional newspapers celebrating match-stick models of cathedrals, palaces, ships. We have gasped in awe at the sheer detail, wondered at the years of striking, trimming and gluing that goes into such ventures. But this is the age of the pallet, and 'Pallet Crafts' have yet to produce their masterworks. Where is the pallet Chartres Cathedral, the pallet Taj Mahal?

Hotels

Because no one, or, at least, very few people actually live in the edgelands, many of these areas lead a double life. Business parks will fill up during office hours, then empty of cars at dusk, leaving the smoked-glass buildings to cleaners and security guards. Warehouses are locked and all the trucks are either out on the road or parked until the morning. Then the streets between the warehouses become the domain of boy racers in their jacked-up rides.

Retail parks are different. They will often stay alive all evening, drawing in shoppers after work, offering them sustenance from Pizza Hut or Starbucks, or chestnuts or hot dogs from barrows off the set of *My Fair Lady*. But perhaps the strangest night-time edgelands is the National Exhibition Centre, just down the road from Birmingham International Airport. Part-retail, part-entertainment, part-residential, this complex needs a category all its own. For a start, it's vast, incorporating acre upon acre of car parks and exhibition halls.

And there are hotels, too, new hotels with their own massive car parks, hotels for business people. In the evening, out of season, these hotels are oddly remarkable.

*

The Premier Inn near the NEC is suitably large and rather attractively landscaped, with trees and grass banks, and picnic tables set out in front of the hotel. Like any Premier Inn (as Lenny Henry will tell you) it is well appointed, quiet and comfortable. When there's a big-name gig at the NEC, or a major show of clothes or cars, this place is buzzing, but go there in late summer before the autumn calendar kicks off, and the Premier Inn is an oasis in a desert.

It is not empty. These places are never empty. There are always sales reps on the road, visitors to nearby edgelands businesses. The restaurant is busy in the evening, and the bar is full of groups of colleagues gossiping away from the office, or lone travellers nursing a drink as they watch the European football or the rolling news on one of the many screens dotted around the bar. There are many screens, and many people watch them, because many people are in a party of one. They have eaten dinner alone, and will be drinking alone, but rather than sit in your room, you may as well enjoy a sense of community by drinking in the bar and watching the football. Those who don't like football, or those who have a presentation in the morning, pore over their laptops on the low bar tables.

Tonight, the bar has a scattering of antiques dealers, here for a small off-season exhibition at the NEC. Earlier in the afternoon they were unloading paintings, boxes of porcelain and statuettes from the backs of estate cars and 4 x 4s. Some are on their own. Some are married couples and business partners, sitting over dinner discussing the effects of the credit crunch, how people don't have the money they used to have to spend on antiques. But if the item is good, and the price is right, you can still make a living.

*

All this is familiar to anyone who stays in hotels aimed at business travellers. But go outside, take a walk, and it's a different story. Walk past the smokers in their shelter near the car park. Walk past the picnic tables and the space-age bike sheds (a laudable nod to the environment, but who cycles here?), now walk out into the middle of the huge and largely empty car park.

Outside, above, around, are miles of nothingness. The sky is clear and you can see hundreds of stars. If you were staying in a city you would step out on to a street, perhaps a street full of restaurants and bars. If you were staying in a hotel in the Highlands you might step out into silence with the mountains bearing down on you in darkness. But this is a different wilderness. Midlands edgelands wilderness. It has the echoing silence of miles of empty car parks, dark and locked glass offices, pockets of woodland and strips of standing water.

If you stand still you can hear the distant roar of a motorway, but few cars loop these edgelands roundabouts at night. This is true remoteness. You could get lost here. All the roads look the same here in the dark, all the roundabouts landscaped and primped. Pavements are few and far between. It feels like the middle of nowhere. It feels like a place 'where a thought might grow', another one for the inventory in the contemporary Irish poet Derek Mahon's magisterial poem 'A Disused Shed in Co. Wexford', alongside 'Peruvian mines, worked out and abandoned', 'Indian compounds where the wind dances', and of course the disused shed itself. The poem is a celebration of the overlooked, the marginal, in this case a long-forgotten shed with its own community of mushrooms unseen for half a century. Fittingly, the shed in question is located as:

Deep in the grounds of a burnt-out hotel,
Among the bathtubs and the washbasins
A thousand mushrooms crowd to a keyhole.
This is the one star in their firmament
Or frames a star within a star.
What should they do there but desire?
So many days beyond the rhododendrons
With the world waltzing in its bowl of cloud,
They have learnt patience and silence
Listening to the rooks querulous in the high wood.

*

Edgelands hotels test a truism of the spaces we all move through in today's world. According to the script, the hotel lobby is one more familiar, undifferentiated space in a chain of spaces that transported you there: airport, transfer bus, taxi. You could be anywhere: the piped muzak, carefully appointed sofas, six-foot yucca plants, the multiple clocks telling you what time it is in distant cities. The real thrill of a lobby is the stepping outside from it. Abroad, this might involve the legendary 'oven-door effect' of unseasonal temperatures, the smells of jasmine or two-stroke, the blare of impatient car horns and the fizz of scooters, but even at home the effect of stepping out into an unfamiliar city, joining the flow and taking your bearings from new buildings and landmarks, can supply a little jolt of strangeness and difference. But in the edgelands, more often than not, a strange thing happens when you step outside: you've been here before. This car park. This row of pot plants. These grassy verges and that sound of water running somewhere. In the edgelands hotel, the lobby extends seamlessly outside into the surroundings.

*

The Premier Inn Swindon West is missing a trick. There is no array of time-zone clocks behind the reception desk. What an opportunity to reference the local, far more intelligently and seductively than any number of shiny leaflets, by presenting a display of local railway times. Forget New York, Paris and Tokyo: Swindon was a rail town, and the Great Western Railway made the first attempt, in 1840, to synchronise local times and apply Greenwich Mean Time as a standard. Before this, towns in England set their own times – local time – adjusted periodically to take into account seasonality and longitude; as the railways grew, stationmasters began to adjust clocks using tables supplied by the train companies, but what was really needed was a syncing-up of the rapidly expanding (and accelerating) network. In an age when travel between towns and cities was conducted using coaches and horsepower, journeys were relatively slow, and the small time discrepancies involved made little difference. The train changed all that, and the electric telegraph meant network synchronisation became possible. Time – or at least our modern conception of it – was invented here, with the timetable. So: London, Slough, Reading, Newbury . . . Clocks set minutes apart, in honour of Swindon's railway past. They could even roll it out across the chain: a novelty reintroduction of pre-industrial time.

*

What is generic? Step back in time. A few coaching inns still stand, usually in England's prettier market towns, but beyond the scuff and abrasion of time, the texture of age, the horse brasses and dubious claim that Charles Dickens once stayed overnight there, they all . . . well, they all look the same. Stamford in Lincolnshire has a good one, the George. Look beyond the modern appurtenances, the reinvented, relaxed, informal eatery and business centre, and there are two rooms still marked 'London' and 'York'; depending on whether you were headed north or south along the Great North Road, this was where you waited for the horses to be changed. Over time, the functionality and tedium of travel becomes part of a lost past. We forget the nine hours it took to travel the ninety miles south to London.

Before the post-war boom in car ownership, many English towns joined by the railway – Newcastle, York, Hull, Carnforth, Bath – had their Royal Station Hotels. Hull's is now the Quality Hotel Royal, described in Philip Larkin's 'Friday Night at the Royal Station Hotel':

> Light spreads darkly downwards from the high
> Clusters of lights over empty chairs
> That face each other, coloured differently.
> Through open doors, the dining-room declares
> A larger loneliness of knives and glass
> And silence laid like carpet. A porter reads
> An unsold evening paper. Hours pass,
> And all the salesmen have gone back to Leeds,
> Leaving full ashtrays in the Conference Room.
>
> In shoeless corridors, the lights burn. How
> Isolated, like a fort, it is –
> The headed paper, made for writing home
> (If home existed) letters of exile: *Now*
> *Night comes on. Waves fold behind villages.*

Larkin is said to have used the Royal Station Hotel as useful neutral ground for meeting visitors to Hull, newly arrived off the train at Paragon Station just around the corner. It doesn't seem as if much has changed in the English travel hotel.

*

As connoisseurs of edgelands hotels, we have visited our share of Premier Inns and Travelodges. But there is something emblematic about the Premier Inn in Swindon West. This is the west end of what used to be called the 'M4 corridor'. From here through Berkshire into London was a hothouse of new business in the Eighties and Nineties, hi-tech business in particular. Swindon cast off its macro-engineering past and embraced the micro-engineering future. The old railway works – where some of the greatest engines of the steam age were built – were closed down, refurbished and reopened as an upmarket retail park. Here, designer stores are interspersed with painted and polished chunks of Victorian machinery, captivating like abstract sculptures, but redundant. Well, perhaps not redundant, but re-employed as industrial chic, touchstones of the past to draw the shoppers in. Every now and then, a brass plaque on the wall reminds you that the leather luggage behind glass wasn't always here: 'To your right is located the former brass finisher's shop of the Great Western Railway Works, also known as "T" shop.'

Lydiard Park, a few miles from here, has its own piece of heritage to offer, a Palladian house, once the ancestral home of the Viscounts Bolingbroke. Swindon Corporation rescued it from ruin in the Forties and opened it to the public. More recently, the Heritage Lottery Fund has backed a restoration of the grounds and gardens, and Swindon is rightly proud of this resource.

You can pick up leaflets on the park and house from the Swindon West Premier Inn. That's because, as you sleep in the hotel, lulled by the sound of traffic from the nearby M4 and the A3102, you are sleeping in 'Lydiard Fields'. Ah, Lydiard Fields. It sounds like a pastoral paradise, and indeed it is. The large business park next door to the hotel incorporates a woodland nature trail, and a small landscaped lake with seats alongside it, for the benefit of employees of the large, smoked-glass office blocks.

The hotel here has a bit of everything you'd expect from edgelands: restored and repackaged local history, a business park next door, car showrooms and hypermarkets across the road, towering pylons striding across the road and past the hotel car park, but it has several features that set it apart, too, and one is a facility called 'Touchbase'.

*

Say you are a manager in a business based in Cardiff, and you need to do some team-building with colleagues in Reading, Swindon and Oxford. What do you do? If only you had a boardroom that wasn't in Cardiff, but just alongside the M4, handy for everyone. Welcome to the future.

Generic Meetings Centres are a new edgelands phenomenon. Sure, they are in city centres, too, but they suit the edgelands perfectly. Here, you can hire a room and a facilitator, and team-build by telling your colleagues three things about yourself (two true, one a lie) in a room that looks like a stripped-down board-room, just like yours only without the company logos and award certificates. You can work all morning, step into the 'break-out' area for coffee and sandwiches, and meet other companies working on their team-building in similar boardrooms of varying sizes, then dive back in to yours. Today, it is your boardroom, and the whiteboard has your mission statement on it. Tomorrow it could be software, or snack foods, or ski pants. At the end of the day, you walk ten yards and you are in your hotel, where old-fashioned team-building can continue facilitated by alcohol in the restaurant and bar.

The manager of Touchbase Swindon West seems a little suspicious of us. She shows us different sizes of boardrooms, gives us coffee, goes away to fetch leaflets and price lists. But we haven't told her the name of our company, because we don't have a company. And we don't need a virtual boardroom. We just like the place, sitting in the upstairs break-out area getting coffee out of the machine, as the sun shines across the A3102 through the large windows.

A couple of managers 'break out' of their training days in different rooms to call taxis on their mobiles. It is late afternoon, and sessions are about to wind up. Those who can spare a night away will walk across to the hotel to start their revelry. The signs on their doors tell us that one man works in the power business, and the other in computers. As we sip our coffee and they order their cabs, an aeroplane – low and loud – crosses the large window, and we all look out. But that's another story.

*

Could edgelands hotels play host to other, less business-minded gatherings? One way of examining our routine prejudices when it comes to landscape and environment is to consider the way creative residential courses are offered. Say you're an aspiring writer. A five-day course in the middle of nowhere with a group of like-minded students, sharing the household chores and taking part in workshops, surrounded by rolling hills, cows, streams, woodland? It's a successful formula. The Arvon Foundation has been running such courses since the Sixties, and now has three centres in England: at Totleigh Barton near Sheepwash in Devon, Lumb Bank near Hebden Bridge in Yorkshire, and the Hurst near Clun in Shropshire. Notice how all these places are 'near' somewhere, and somewhere pretty remote at that.

But why can't courses in poetry or writing a novel or screen-writing happen at Swindon West? We think it could work. There'd be no fretting over room-sharing or doors with no locks on them; no sulky spud-peeling over the organic bin; no guilt over not taking full advantage of the lovely walking on offer; no poems about the way sheep stare at you. Evening meals would mean jolly gather-ings in the neighbouring Brewer's Fayre for some 'pub classics', where, on the final evening the group reading could take place, much to the bemusement of a few Support Analysts and Development Managers, who will wonder what all the shouting is about and why the sound has been turned down on the televisions.

*

The writing centre at the Hurst used to be the home of the play-wright John Osborne, who once described Brighton as having a smell of spunk in its air. He was referring to Brighton's prowess as a venue for the dirty weekend. Once again, we can hold our prej-udices up to the light. A dirty weekend in an edgelands hotel: is that possible? We know it isn't desirable. And yet.

We wouldn't be surprised if Tebay Hotel and Services in Cumbria became a haven for fugitive couples. Already known to many travel-ling on the northern stretches of the M6 as 'those different services', Tebay manages to stand out in the memory of the tired driver as something of an oasis. In the edgelands between England and Scotland, its picture windows look out across bleak but beautiful north Lakeland fells, and its cafeteria – surrounded by a pond with ducks – gives the impression that you are drinking your coffee on a small island in the middle of Ullswater.

Now that English couples no longer have to escape to Scotland to marry across the border at Gretna Green, we would like to propose Tebay's hotel (tucked a hundred yards behind the services) as a suitable location for eloping (or even long-standing) couples. After all, rustic hotels are nice, but you'll need a good navigator or a satnav, and eloping couples don't have time for that. And with city hotels there's always the risk of meeting that nosy old bloke from accounts, who's here on business and wonders exactly what your business is. No, Tebay is in the middle of nowhere, but only two minutes off the M6, so for busy couples wishing to hide out from angry relatives or endless, repetitive election coverage on the TV, Tebay is the new Gretna Green, indeed, the new Brighton.

*

Edgelands are constantly shifting and being redeveloped. That's part of what makes them dynamic, hard to pin down. Some crop up in pockets close to city centres, where waste ground and industrial decline has offered space for the edgelands to self-seed.

Swindon West edgelands are the classic form – right on the fringe, on the border where urban and rural meet. If you leave the hotel car park and turn left, you head in – through a sequence of identical-looking roundabouts – towards the town itself, with its sprawling estates and clusters of old railwayman's cottages. Turn right out of the hotel and you are on your way to rural England, Wiltshire-style. And one of the first small towns you reach in this direction is Wootton Bassett.

It is strange to see how a place name that meant little to anyone outside Wiltshire a year ago could now be so heavy with meaning and emotion. RAF Lyneham is the reason, or, more specifically, Afghanistan is the reason. Wootton Bassett's long, straight, picturesque high street is now a familiar sight on the news, as locals and visitors carry out a new and moving ritual. No one seems to know why silence wasn't working here, but it wasn't. So people started to applaud and throw flowers as the funeral cortèges passed, bearing British soldiers killed in the latest fighting in Helmand. Those soldiers almost certainly flew out from Lyneham, and they come back here, too, only some come back in body bags.

Everybody knows this. That's why, when an RAF Hercules lumbers low across the edgelands here, people pause and watch. Cars slow down. Businessmen falter in their phone calls.

Retail

Think of *Little House on the Prairie*, if you can bear it. Now extend that thought to any farm in rural America as mediated to us by TV, movies, breakfast-cereal packets and cartoons. The sun is setting, and the rooster is roosting. The cornucopia is gathered in, and the family settles down to say grace before the evening meal. Where is the crop? Safely in the groaning, barrel-bellied, mighty barn across the yard from the farmhouse, with its doors firmly barred shut and the cats sleeping soundly, and so on, and so on . . .

Cut to the outskirts of Birmingham, or Swindon, or almost any English town. Here, in the edgelands retail parks, that breadbasket rustic vernacular style is played out in the form of supermarkets, hypermarkets and ubermarkets. Many of these brimful barns even have the clock on the top of their turret, so the workers in the fields know when to come in for their tea.

These giant warehouse-shops are only possible in edgelands. They take up too much space to sit in the middle of towns. City department stores are different, like town houses with their central stairs and lifts, themed floors and carpeted walkways. Edgelands retail barns rarely have one upper floor, let alone many. They don't need them. Who needs height when you can lay out your wares on a floor space the size of a small farm?

*

But groaning barns are not the only theme employed in retail parks. In Birmingham's Fort Shopping Park the shoppers are invited to consider themselves at sea. Here, the architecture subtly suggests a dockside row of chandlers, with the 'anchor store' rising above the others, showing more than a hint of funnel and prow.

The maritime theme is taken to a new level at the Trafford Centre, outside Manchester, one of England's biggest retail parks, sitting in the middle of one of England's richest edgelands. Here, as you cruise north-west along the M60 heading for Barton Bridge, you see the Manchester Ship Canal cutting its wide swathe through the flatlands to the west, and to the east a massive sports store, a covered dry ski slope like a vast wedge of cheese towering above the motorway, a sewage works, a set of allotments, and the Trafford Centre at the heart of it all.

The Trafford Centre from the M60 – especially at night – is like a distant Samarkand or Byzantium. Its great domes, turrets and pillars are protected by statues of ancient gods and goddesses. Inside, the opulence continues. Elaborate fountains feature golden dolphins spouting roof-high jets of water for the sheer joy of being here. Walls alongside stairs and escalators depict sylvan scenes in which the god Pan shares enchanted woodlands with various founders and fundraisers of the shopping centre.

But all this is just the antechamber. At the heart of the Trafford Centre the classical pagan theme gives way to a thematic cacophony. As you leave the shops to enter the food hall, you pass through an Italian village, with people sitting out at tables under the electrically starlit night sky. Waiters scurry in and out of fabricated trattorias, complete with upstairs windows, juliet balconies and imitation creepers clinging to the walls.

Keep going and you walk out on to the deck of a colossal ocean liner under a cloudless, fake night sky. If this feels too much like the *Titanic*, you can dart down one of many side alleys, offering not just that Italian village experience, but a similarly themed walk through Chinese, or Greek, or ancient Egyptian streets.

This is Disney's Epcot landed in south Manchester, and it fits the edgelands perfectly. Here there is space to play, to build what could never be imagined in a city centre. This is retail as entertainment and spiritual experience. Where other retail parks are subtle in their metaphors of cornucopian abundance, or voyages of discovery, the Trafford Centre goes the whole way. It is nothing short of a temple to retail. Perhaps that should be disturbing. Maybe we should be shocked at what such a place says about *fin de siècle* British culture. But instead it is beguiling in its honesty. After all, every religion should have its great cathedrals, and the worship of Mammon is no exception.

*

If the Trafford Centre shows retail packaged as entertainment, Birmingham's Star City shows that entertainment can be packaged as retail. Star City is well signposted for miles around, and it needs to be, because it sits beneath the complex of intersecting motorways and A-roads that cross just south of the city centre, the edgelands between centre and suburbs. From the name, it sounds like another shopping centre or factory outlet, but this is in fact a palace of pleasure. As is fitting for the edgelands, themes are mixed and matched here – jungle, space, sport, Americana – and it runs all day and evening, feeding and entertaining groups from families to young couples to children's parties. On the roof of the building – in a rooftop compound with very high fences – football partygoers step out into the elements and play five-a-side as cars scream past on the nearby flyover.

But if you don't like football, or you don't like the weather, you could always stay indoors and shoot people. The edgelands are a very good place to go if you like shooting people. This is not a word of advice to urban gangsters to head out to the edgelands when there's business to be done. We're talking paintballs and lasers here, not bullets. And at Star City, it's lasers.

Λ laser arena is top of many children's list of party venues, but as with any kind of shooting game, it's really aimed at adults. For those who haven't experienced the joys of safe kills, here's how it generally goes in your local laser venue. You check in and pay your money, then you enter an antechamber where you get tooled up. This involves donning something like a bulletproof vest, only with more bells, whistles and lights on it. And, of course, you get your laser gun, which makes you feel like one of the Imperial Guard in *Star Wars*. It must be stressed, for the benefit of the sceptics, that this feels good. It may feel very foolish if you were tooled up in this way in your office, or in the restaurants dotted around the complex, but in here, where everyone is similarly attired, it feels good.

Now you enter the killing zone, which is a large, darkened room (or sometimes a series of rooms) with different levels of runways, walls and boxes like shadowy buildings, ramps and vantage points. Every time you shoot someone, a sensor on their laser vest lights up, right above the solar plexus. This is very satisfying. But if someone shoots you, your own solar plexus lights up and vibrates. This is very distressing. When your allotted time is up, you and your group leave the killing zone, and as you disrobe, your scores are flashed up on a screen. For every kill you made, points are added to your total. But points are taken off for every hit you take.

For stag nights and sixteenth, seventeenth, eighteenth birthday parties this all gets tactical and very competitive. For younger kids it's a raucous affair, with lots of rushing around firing random shots into the darkness. Except for the dads. The dads have taken up sniper positions in the highest corners of the killing zone. From here, they can ensure they keep a clean sheet, picking off their children's friends to guarantee victory.

There's a story of a dad returning from his son's laser party to his sympathetic wife. She had not been in favour of a shooting party, but their son wanted it so much that she gave way. After all, it's only lasers.

'It must have been difficult to play the game,' she said, 'knowing you had to point a gun at ten-year-old boys.'

'Not really,' said the dad, 'you just aim lower.'

*

The retail park has an upstart younger sibling – the outlet village. These are not just shopping centres, they bill themselves as 'experiences'. This is where retail park shades into theme park. The philosopher Jean Baudrillard defined hyperreality as 'the simulation of something which never really existed'. Although he probably wrote that line between drags on a Gauloises in the corner of a café on La Rive Gauche, the penny might have dropped even sooner had he sipped an espresso bought from a barrow pushed by a man in authentic street-vendor costume at an English outlet village.

These are special places. Cheshire Oaks Designer Outlet Village in Ellesmere Port is our 'local'. But we fancy a bit of an adventure, so one weekend we head south. As we stroll through the quaint streets of Bicester Outlet Village in Oxfordshire, a short drive from the M40, we feel distinctly underdressed. The beautiful people are out to restock their wardrobes on a dazzling Sunday afternoon.

And it does feel like a village – of sorts. Its own publicity describes it thus: 'Designed in the vernacular of traditional Oxfordshire rural architecture with individually defined boutique stores facing an open-air, landscaped pedestrianised mall, Bicester Village recalls the ambience of south-east England villages.' But one man's ambience is another man's pastiche. It is a version of the past that seems authentic, because it never existed. And in keeping with the American roots of the 'outlet village' concept, there's a touch of New England here too. It's a cross between *Cider with Rosie* and Martha's Vineyard.

But it works. We buy things. After all, if a good outlet village offers an experience beyond mere shopping, and if its hyperreality is akin to walking round a film set, then maybe our wallets are hyperreal, too, and what we do with money in 'the village' doesn't necessarily connect with the world outside. So why the poetic air of melancholia? There's a sadness to these places,. A successful pastiche makes us feel nostalgic for something we never knew, a past we never experienced. Struck by a nameless sense of loss, we stop for a hazelnut latte outside a timber-fronted Oxfordshire cottage selling designer stilettos.

*

As the M62 tapers down and funnels traffic into Liverpool's edgelands, you pass through a boulevard of retail. Car showrooms, tile centres, leather worlds, carpet empires and fast-food bars come thick and fast, and with them come the flags and inflatables. This same scene – even with many of the same brands – is replicated on the roads into Manchester, London, Birmingham. But these are not flags to kill or die for. These are flags competing for your attention, an urgent but empty semaphore of bright colours, smiley faces, company logos and special offers. Alongside them, tethered mini-airships tell you to pull in for a bargain, and towering inflatable cartoon men with arms outstretched shimmer and sway in a pose of fixed ecstasy, as if caught at the moment they discovered just how good a zimbamburger actually tastes.

Of course, this flag-fest does no harm. Most of us drive through it all and rarely, if ever, pull in to explore what's being sold. But maybe this is better than simply harmless? Maybe these edgelands chroma-cacophonies are subtly inoculating us against the extremes that flags can represent? Perhaps these long streets of new, empty flags will gradually weaken the power of the old flags, robbing them of their specific potency by sheer weight of numbers. If so, then let's see more. Let every edgelands road in every city in every country become a boulevard of pointless, garish, wind-blown spectacle.

Business

In from the villages or out from the towns, every morning cars thread and reel their way around the roundabouts of edgelands business parks, to go to work. You can't get here by train, but driving works because the edgelands are a driver's dream – few queues, long, straight roads and ample parking.

But the parking isn't public. Nothing in a business park is public. There are no parks or playing fields, no common ground. Each business has its own parking around it, and the success of the business is reflected in the number of parking spaces. Large, thriving hi-tech companies squat in glass palaces, surrounded by rows of orderly parking spaces, cordoned off by tidy well-trimmed flower beds. You can park here if you have a staff permit. If not, your car will be removed and humanely destroyed. Well, your car will be taken to pieces and reused as building materials for new business parks.

There are, outside the bigger buildings, a handful of visitors' parking spaces, but you need to get a pass from reception/security, and you need an appointment. No one visits without an appointment, because no one is just passing. You come to these business parks to do business. There is no other reason to drive here. At the edge of the business parks are the multi-occupancy buildings occupied by companies on their way up, or down. For these fledgling or failing businesses each parking space is a significant monthly expense. They are numbered, and fiercely defended. If a visitor parks in a paid-for, sweated-over space, then a line has been crossed, and vengeance will be swift.

*

Today in a business park in the English Midlands the sun is low and sharp. Teams of gardeners tend the beds that surround glass offices. But the shrubs and flowers don't just decorate perimeters, they read like spreadsheets. Thriving businesses have bigger teams of gardeners with better equipment – ride-on mowers, leaf-blowers – and more extravagant floral displays.

One software company has a small lake on the corner of its plot, on the junction of two identical arterial roads. The lake is surrounded by bulrushes. Willows weep into its shallows. There may be fish, but no one fishes here. And nobody walks by the lake, no pavements or paths trace its banks. It is there to be seen from a distance, by car, or from the high, smoked-glass office windows. Code-crunchers, strategists and accountants are meant to glance out between tasks, catch sight of the company lake, and be reminded that their business is a big fish, a veritable great white in a world of minnows. At the side of the lake is a sign – visible from the road – warning that the water is deep, and no one should risk it, should take its depth for granted. This is no shallow pool for show: it has fathoms, darkness. This is serious water for a serious business. Across the road from the deep-water sign is another warning – this one for drivers – with a silhouette of a stag suggesting that deer from the wild woods nearby might leap into the path of a car on its way to do business.

This 'deer in the road' warning sign means one thing for drivers, and another for poets. There's a popular myth (perpetuated by poets who are serial driving-test failures) that poets can't – even shouldn't – drive. Not only is this untrue, but it's pernicious. Because driving is a fundamentally poetic activity – ritualistic, solipsistic, liberating. And great poets not only drive, they write about driving. How many Seamus Heaney poems begin or end in a car? Whether travelling at night through the French countryside, or skirting the coast in his native Northern Ireland, Heaney is a poetic driver, as poems from throughout his writing life – 'The Peninsula', 'Night Drive', 'On the Road', 'Postscript' – attest. In fact, he even composes poems while driving, tapping out the beat of a line on top of his steering wheel. Les Murray has written about his own landscape as seen through the windscreen of a car in his 'Portrait of the Artist as New World Driver':

> Delight of a stick shift –
> Farms were abandoned for these pleasures. Second
> To third in this Mazda is a stepped inflection
> Third back to first at the lights
> A concessive
> V of junction.

But if driving poems are a genre, then there's a significant subgenre of roadkill poems. To be more specific still, there should be an anthology of deer-roadkill poems. William Stafford kills his pregnant doe on a mountain road. Frances Leviston meets hers at dusk, and the collision reveals 'what is not meant to be seen' – the innards of the fatally wounded animal. Such is the potency of these deer-kill poems, that one young poet admitted – in the bar after a reading – to driving carelessly down woodland roads in the hope of being hit by a poem. This is a dangerous game, since deer are large and solid, and a poet should know that you can't court or coax the muse anyway. John Berryman infamously wished catastrophic illness upon himself, in the hope that it would fuel his 'Dream Songs'. But his best *Dream Songs* came at times of calm lucidity.

Perhaps one day a stag will stumble out into this Midlands edgelands road and, frightened by a car, will leap the low hedge and dive into the company lake. Who would notice? Who would write the poem? But today there is no stag. Here on this bold, bright morning as the gardeners tend their corporate beds, the future seems good. Recession or no, this business park, with mock-Neolithic stone circles in the middle of its roundabouts, seems permanent and confident. Cars come and go, as employees blink in the dazzle between tinted glass of car and office. By the huge bins at the back of one office, a woman in high heels sweeps an aerosol across a bouquet of dried flowers, painting them gold.

*

The 'M4 corridor' was always an evocative idea. In the Eighties it became synonymous with England's burgeoning digital economy. Driving out of London in your gold Mark III Capri, you flew past Windsor, Staines, Slough, Reading, Newbury, on towards Swindon, with Go West's eponymous debut album putting your speakers through their paces. If silicon had a smell, you might wind down the window, let the wind ruffle your perm, sample the metallic tang of early mobile phones, early computers, the scent of a new age.

In truth, it should have been called the Kennet and Avon corridor. From the M4 all you got was a glimpse of edgelands riches as you shot past them: the gravel pits near Reading, the mast of the Membury transmitter towering above the motorway services like a cathedral spire. Most of the new business parks were tucked away down slip roads, behind landscaped verges, visible only in the tilt of bright red roof. But if you took a walk down the towpath of the Kennet and Avon Canal you got a different view. Here – like John Constable's vistas in Dedham Vale – was the alchemy of water, fields and buildings on a flat plain. But the buildings here were more exotic than a mill, or a distant village church. The new business parks of the Eighties were brash in colour and style, often bright red and worlds apart from the local brick and flint vernacular. If they looked like any other buildings, they were bastard children of the tractor shed, the Lego castle and the pagoda, with a touch of influence from the late-Seventies alien classic *Close Encounters of the Third Kind*. There was no attempt here to conjure the *genius loci*, rather an expansive sense of confidence. The future was being forged here in England, in the garish business parks along the Kennet and Avon corridor.

*

At the insistence of planners, and with the assistance of environmental artists, the *genius loci* is back in fashion. In an uncertain age, with a volatile economy and ecology, Noughties business parks lack the chutzpah of their Eighties forebears. Under the skin, these buildings are the same as ever, steel frames designed for quick and cheap assembly. These are often generic boxes, with internal walls designed for easy dismantling, to reshape the workspace within, as business fortunes rise and fall. But once the steel frame is up, a skin is selected to reflect something of the genius loci. In an area noted for its half-timbered buildings, business parks will wear a little black and white. If the local stone is granite, then the offices may get a granite skin, though costs may mean the stone is sourced from China. Before a foundation is laid, the ecologists and archae-ologists have combed the site, but the faux Neolithic stone circles are generally the work of local artists, brought in by the planners to help the new business park to 'bed in' to the environment.

*

Many of the panel-skins on business park buildings have a thirty-year life expectancy. These are not like the Victorian canal-side mills, robust enough to be reborn as offices and loft apartments. What will become of the business parks? As planners try to shore up the economic life of England's inner cities and towns, these parks may have to reinvent themselves, be re-skinned as low-cost housing. A few generations down the line, when the 'doughnut effect' (empty town centres with a ring of business and retail parks on the outskirts) has gone into reverse, the silence of business parks will be broken. Step out of your car on the forecourt of a smoked-glass office block today and you hear nothing but the wind in the newly planted indigenous shrubs, and the barely audible hum of a surveil-lance camera turning to get a good look at you. Scroll forward three decades and children will be playing football in the former car parks, parents pushing prams past the stone circle to the feature pond with broken fountain. But they might have to lay some pavements first.

Ranges

By day, the many golf driving ranges that have cropped up on the outskirts of Britain's towns and cities in the last several decades look far from enticing. These are usually dull, shed-like constructions; extended sheds, since they stretch far enough to cover the width of a large field.

Walk inside and you find a glittering selection of this season's golf clubs, plus an array of weatherproof trousers, branded shirts and caps. Most punters take no notice of these, they walk straight to the desk and speak a number: 25, 50, 100. Money changes hands, and in return, a slip of paper with a code number on it. Through another door, then you enter the range. A machine on the wall spits out the number of balls you have bought into a plastic basket, then you choose your bay and start hitting. Er, that's it.

*

Except, except, by night these driving ranges change . . .

It is early evening, midweek in winter, just past the rush hour. The traffic is beginning to thin out as you leave the city, and your eye is drawn to the horizon, to a blinding light. Is it a crashed meteor? You see no flames. Is it a nuclear explosion? You see no mushroom cloud. Is it an international airport? You see no planes. A few miles and minutes closer, it reveals itself as a set of hugely powerful floodlights mounted on the roof of a long, low building. You peel off the dual carriageway and follow the signs. You drive through an empty business park, glancing at the buildings to see if anyone's working later than you. Out between the offices you hit an unlit road, with Shangri-La at the end of it, a shining symbol of release and recreation in the middle of the edgelands.

You came here on spec, without any golf clubs, so you hire a seven iron and a driver and you pay for fifty balls. You choose a bay, and the men – for it is almost invariably men at this hour – on either side of you give you a nod of acknowledgement. You take off your suit jacket, hang it on the peg provided, loosen your tie, roll up your shirtsleeves. Then you look out at the targets, floodlit in front of you, a field dotted with yardage signs. There are greens, too, raised banks with different coloured flags on. The field is peppered with white golf balls. At the back – well beyond the 250 sign – is a tall mesh fence. Beyond that, the business park, the road, and beyond all of them the city you have left behind.

And so you join this silent ritual. No one says a word. Everyone came here alone. This is not about hitting. Anyone who has been to a driving range knows that trying to hit the ball hard invariably ends in disaster – a gunshot crack as the ball shoots off the toe of your club into the wooden wall of your bay. No, this is all about timing, rhythm, letting the club-head do the work. You came to hit some shots, but now you are part of a larger ritual. The rain starts. It pelts down on the corrugated roof above you. And out there, slow white bullets trace an arc across the sky, spinning right to left or left to right, crossing each other in the air. Six, seven, ten at a time, out into the night.

*

Some of the larger ranges have two decks of bays, which allows for even more elaborate cross-hatch patterns. And what is it for? Supposedly, these places were set up for golfers to work on their swings when they didn't have time (or it was too dark) to go out on the golf course. But this isn't about golf at all. Many of the punters here are strangers to golf courses, others used to play on courses, but found themselves drawn more and more to this place instead. On a golf course you play a shot, then you walk after it. You face the consequences of your swing when you have to play the next shot from the sand or heather where your ball came to rest. At the range, there are no such consequences. Half the time, there are so many balls in the air you cannot tell which is yours.

This range ritual has more in common with yoga or dance than it does with golf. You come away having helped to make great shapes in the floodlit sky. Your role in this was to turn up, receive your basket of shiny white objects, then propel them out into the ether. Once you have sent them all on their way, you step aside, and someone else can take your bay. The volunteers change throughout the night, but the ritual, the pattern-making, continues. If this had been dreamt up by Mark Wallinger or Gillian Wearing it would be in the running for the Turner Prize.

*

There is something inherently cinematic about the driving range, especially at night. Maybe it's the glare of the floodlights, lending the scene ahead of you the air of a set; or the distance markers, turning the teed-up, close-up of the ball into a long shot, a focus-puller's nightmare. There have been driving ranges in American movies since Fred Astaire danced and balanced his way through a run of syncopated tee shots in *Carefree*, but more recently the driving range has been a place where characters can meet privately to talk off the record – as Alec Baldwin and Matt Damon do in Scorsese's *The Departed* – or as a shadier, noirish venue: in *The Insider* Russell Crowe finds a deserted driving range both a venue for a lonely underlining of his own will and resolution, but also a threatening space when another golfer appears several tees away to echo his own drives out into the dark. The driving range might even come to find itself a noir trope in cinematic scenery – like the underground car park – where shadows gather in the edge of our field of vision.

*

As you drive out of the car park you feel you have achieved something, but you're not sure what it was. You glance sideways as you accelerate down the side of the field, and you see the patterns again from a new angle. As you pass the very end of the field, where the power of the floodlights wanes to little more than a moonlight gloss, you see some flecks of white in the long grass beyond the 250 sign, beyond the 300, over the back fence into the scrublands. These flecks are signs of a great mystery, the moment when the timing of a swing worked to such perfection that the ball arced out beyond the pattern, into hyperspace. These are the miracle moments a man lives for.

Lights

In the middle years of the last decade a photographer called Henry
Iddon took to lugging his gear into the Westmoreland and Cumbrian
hills of the Lake District region, climbing high into the dusk and
screwing his camera to a tripod on the tops of Coniston Old Man,
Black Coombe, Thornthwaite Beacon, Helm Crag, Skiddaw, Whin
Rigg, to wait for nightfall, and the onset of the darkest hours. Above
an invisible auditory ceiling, the soft roar of road traffic fades away,
to be replaced by the wind, Herdwick sheep and the occasional cry
of a bird as the nightshift takes over. The long-exposure images he
made on those journeys captured the darkness and stillness of the
fells, the deep ground of the image cauterised here and there by the
hot weld of car headlights cutting the path of a main road, or the
hotel glare from the tourist honeypots.

But when Iddon opened the shutter for those brief seconds and
allowed the night in, he sometimes also caught the distant towns
and cities. In the Coniston Old Man image, the camera is pointing
south, across towards the Westmoreland coast, Morecambe Bay
and the Fylde beyond, though translated into this heightened
digital world the lowlands where people live and work look like
roiling lava fields, the glowing coals of the distant roads and street
lamps and floodlit car parks and retail centres. It's like seeing the
ghost of heavy industry, its long-extinguished blast furnaces and
smelting plants and ironworks, all fired up and working again.

The edgelands must lie somewhere between this Romantic night and that crucible of molten tungsten, sodium and halogen.

> I have been one acquainted with the night.
> I have walked out in rain – and back in rain.
> I have outwalked the furthest city light.

Robert Frost's lyric 'Acquainted with the Night' suggests an archetypal early twentieth-century urban edge: one last symbol of civility and order in the form of a street lamp burning on the road that leads beyond the outskirts. As such roads become lanes, their last high-walled houses hold on to the only sources of artificial light, beneath a strong moon that outshines all beneath it: the late nineteenth-century of Atkinson Grimshaw. Beyond this, all is night.

In early twenty-first-century England, such darkness is much harder to find. There are three kinds of light pollution: 'sky glow' is the aura visible above our urban areas, amplified by water droplets in the air and other particulate matter; 'glare' is the fixed and intense brightness created by golf driving ranges or distribution centres or rail maintenance gangs; 'light trespass' is the general leakage of artificial light from badly designed street lamps or security lamps. Light itself has become toxic.

*

What does the edgelands night look like? Looking up, a cloudy night can give back anything from a muddy orange to a bruised magenta, with many nuances of pink and red and brown in between. It's the colour of an artist's palette, if the different pigments are overworked and allowed to blend together into a warm grey sludge. A meatpaste sky. Gentleman's Relish.

Depending on where you are in relation to a city centre, one horizon might offer a roseate aura. Sometimes, a compass rose of light can surround you in this way, the glow of several cities. Clear nights can bring a few stars to the edgelands, though the best places to see those are unlit sites of dereliction that our motorways and business corridors have bypassed. Walking past the scrap-metal yards and among the long timber sheds on an industrial estate, with the nearest city centre a few miles away, our stargazing was constantly interrupted by security light. Even when finding a negative oasis of darkness, it's difficult to see the *shades* of stars, their spectral colours, and to feel the size and scale of the night.

On the ground, the edgelands are full of places that can flare up suddenly as if lit by a Very light over no-man's-land. A fox patrolling the perimeters of its nocturnal beat trips the motion sensor on a halogen security light, flooding a loading bay on an industrial estate in a huge and pointless brightness. The fox freezes, its fear and vigilance recorded on CCTV and written in to the cobalt platter of a hard drive.

'The newer the culture is, the more it fears nightfall,' wrote the German journalist and historian Wolfgang Schivelbusch. There are many ghosts in the edgelands' never-quite-dark. Post-industrial England is haunted by a future that never happened, and the inescapable truth that these are the results of our long reclamation of the night: a blackbird singing at midnight on a floodlit roundabout; the silvery lake surface of a deserted conference centre car park; the steadfast glow of bus-stop advertisements. Ballardian trickledown meant synth pop stars like Gary Numan could posit a future (from a vantage point sometime around 1980) where there would be no street lights, but no dark corners either. In this future that never happened:

All the buildings had lights in the walls, glowing depending on what time of day it was. As it got darker, they would glow brighter and brighter. Constant light, and everything was white. No humans, all machines, so it was clean; no dust, no pollution, nothing.

Thirty years on and this hygienic brilliance never quite materialised. Instead, our cities are threaded and surrounded by a half-lit sprawl. We move through our own murky, night-vision home movies. Driving through edgelands at night can feel like diving onto a wreck.

*

The obsession with security lights on offices and warehouses has taken such a hold that many of us now feel we need them on our homes. In housing estates on the edges of our towns and cities this sets up a strange pattern, a slow Morse conversation between back gardens, with each 'dash' lasting thirty seconds. These give us some comfort. We like them to be working, but how do we act upon them? Do they wake us up? Do they wake anyone up? They offer a useful service to cats, to light up the rodent they are seeking to catch, so the rodent freezes in the halogen glare, giving itself up to the jaws.

Perhaps this suggests another, less publicised, form of light pollution, of a kind that affects poets and lovers in particular. Take Philip Larkin's poem 'Sad Steps', in which the poet 'Groping back to bed after a piss', parts the curtains to look out at the night sky and the gardens, and is 'startled by / The rapid clouds, the moon's cleanliness'. In a beautiful description of a moonlit suburban landscape, Larkin describes:

> Four o'clock: wedge-shadowed gardens lie
> Under a cavernous, a wind-picked sky.

But now those 'wedge-shadowed gardens' would be bathed in daylight-bright halogen, triggered by any passing cat. Moonlight would be hard-pressed to compete.

*

For the insomniac, there might be some cold and baleful comfort to be found in visiting a motorway in the middle of the night. Just standing on a deserted bridge above six illuminated lanes, watching the lorries heading north towards Carlisle or Glasgow, the red tail lights of cars zooming southwards towards Warrington and Birmingham. It's like looking into a river of light, feeling the current of people you can never really know passing through great banks of dark trees and hills. You are not alone. Even a generation ago the country seemed to shut down for the night: the airwaves cleared after the national anthem, the closedown dot melted into the olive ground of the television screen, the milk bottles were put out. We would enter a long tunnel of night. Now, light itself seems to flow swiftly along our major roads, pooling in the backwaters of goods depots and hypermarkets, leaking 24/7 into the texture of our night world.

*

Seen from military satellites, our conurbations are joined up in storm systems of light. The thirty miles between Liverpool and Manchester are some of the most mature edgelands on the planet. The first railways were laid here, over the mossy, scrubby land, and ever since, a strip of development has grown: the giant IKEA superstore at Warrington; the pallet yards at Flixton; the Ship Canal, the East Lancs Road, the M62 corridor. Invisibly, mobile phone cellular coverage extended along these paths to meet at some point in between the urban centres. And on one uncelebrated night in the recent past, the pixel-per-square-kilometre count in the fields and wasteland and goods yards midway between these two cities reached a saturation point that meant both became graphically joined, a bright miasma connecting both.

*

O tungsten, o tungsten, how can a light-bulb filament, an eyelash-fine coil of wire, evoke such loyalty and nostalgia? Is it the warm russet tinge it lends to a room in the evening? Is it the soft ringing sound that tells you a bulb is dead, as you brush it past an ear? Is it the volatility, the sudden 'pop' as the filament breaks? Is it the dusting of black on the inside of the glass left by evaporated tungsten? No wonder tungsten lovers are flocking to buy up the last of the incandescent bulbs, before we make the final switch to low-energy.

How little did the inventors of the light bulb (not just Thomas Edison, but – historians argue – at least twenty-two mavericks who played a part in dreaming up the incandescent light) think that they were also inventing a metaphor for thinking itself. A bulb lights up above the head, and an idea is born. So widely understood is this image that it can be used as a universal graphic shorthand for 'inspiration'. Is that why we lament the loss of the incandescent bulb so much? After all, metaphors can be orphaned by technology. How long will it be before 'cut' and 'paste' refer only to manoeuvres on computer screens, and any reference to paper, scissors and glue is forgotten?

We need not fear. If anything, the metaphor should become more accurate as the technology changes. If a tungsten bulb has (as its proponents often argue) the edge over low-energy alternatives because of its instant 'on' and 'off', then surely it falls down as a metaphor on these same grounds? How do ideas come? Well, mostly they emerge. To borrow a gardening metaphor, you get the seed of an idea in an instant, then it grows as you dwell on it, until it comes to full fruition. If so, that sounds far more like a low-energy bulb. In this case, then, perhaps the technological change will serve to strengthen the metaphor, and we will still be drawing light bulbs (albeit perhaps in a different shape) over people's heads for centuries to come.

*

The artist Richard Billingham is probably best know for the photographs he made of his family, collected in *Ray's a Laugh*, but towards the end of the Nineties he returned to Cradley Heath in the West Midlands and started photographing again. By 2003 he was working on nocturnes:

> I felt a great longing for these little places, street corners, bits of waste ground and brick walls, places that I would play in as a kid or pass through on the way to school or to run an errand for my mom. I also realised my relationship with my home town had begun to change at this time . . . I wanted to see how my relationship to my home town had further changed. This time I decided to take more detailed photographs on a medium-format camera and at night using long exposures. Making much slower work in this way forced a different kind of attention before taking each picture. I also

found that my senses seemed more heightened at night due to the silence and the darkness and the fact that no one else was around.

Billingham's images of the Black Country from this period are arrangements in black and gold, post-industrial Whistlers. Cars parked up for the night; deserted streets; gaps in crumbling walls that lead on to waste ground. The yellowy, sodium light of street lamps is intensified during the long exposures, gilding and burnishing brickwork and pavement. We've all seen these places without really looking at them, but in these photographs, instead of an attempted beautification, the stillness and abandonment of our edgelands at night, in their never-dark, is allowed to slow-burn through.

*

Where there are lights, there are cameras. Artificial light and surveillance have long been associated with one another, even before photography was possible. In fifteenth-century England persons on the street at night were required by law to bear a lit torch, so they might make themselves easily visible. During the French Revolution in 1789 gangs of protesters worked their way through the Paris streets smashing the lanterns they associated with an oppressive regime. These same mobs hanged their victims from street lanterns. Street lighting was seen as a means of control and order. Our cities today are policed with the help of telecoms, lighting and CCTV. The cameras move, guided by toggle switches in monitoring suites: the twenty-first-century panopticons.

*

Remember, Jeremy Bentham's panopticon was never actually built – it was designed by Bentham as a utopian, super-efficient prison in 1785, where the imprisoned would be unable to tell when and if they are being watched, thus creating the illusion of constant surveillance – yet it has become synonymous with surveillance, a model for the way we are overlooked and compromised, subconsciously altering our behaviour accordingly. The figures are terrifying: there is said to be one camera for every fourteen people in the United Kingdom, and an individual might expect to be caught on camera 300 times during an active day in a busy urban setting.

Over the past decade, though, there has been a change in the way we might think of the panopticon. Traditionally, the flow of information was always in favour of the powerful, an Orwellian observing and controlling by a few privileged individuals of less-privileged multitudes. But surveillance happens in so many other ways as well now, to serve so many different purposes, whether those are focus groups being observed by market researchers or real-life police-chase shows, consumption or titillation, military campaigns or domestic deterrence. And the process increasingly seems to cut both ways. For example, the powerful can now routinely find themselves scrutinised and observed in ways unimaginable a generation ago, and the markers and conditions for privacy have shifted.

We begin to consider the edgopticon. It already exists, in parts. Webcams posted on weather stations, updating images of masts and sunshine recorders through a rain-freckled lens every few minutes; a security camera overlooking the glassy expanse of a conference centre car park at night; the fringes of retail parks and power station checkpoints and fences surrounding storage depots, the aprons of petrol station forecourts, all monitored around the clock; braking distances of hard shoulder and grass verge picked up by speed cameras. But the edgopticon still has many more blind spots, places to be invisible.

*

Now we have a complicated relationship with our street lights. The future equivalents of those French revolutionaries smashing street lights might be militant wings (yet to emerge, but imaginable) of anti-pollution protesters, punishing the authorities who have lined the streets with light-polluting devices – too tall, too ill-directed. According to the Campaign for the Protection of Rural England, light pollution in the United Kingdom increased by 24 per cent in the last seven years of the twentieth century.

But equally, our street lights have become nostalgic objects, even symbols of childhood (like the lamp post in Narnia), and some will go to great lengths to keep them. A pensioner in St Andrews, Bristol, chained himself to one of his local 1920s lamp posts to save them, when Bristol City Council came to replace them with new tall steel posts. The council said the old cast-iron lights were too low, too dim, and that the significant levels of car crime in the area could be countered by brighter lighting.

While some councils look to brighten their streets at night, others want the power to dim them. Surrey County Council has decided to replace its 89,000 orange street lights with brighter white lights, but then put them all on a dimmer switch in Guildford, so they can adjust the level of light according to need in different parts of the county.

Recent research by a team of biologists from Bristol University has shown that our passion for brightly lit streets is having a detrimental effect on the lives of bats. Evolution has hard-wired these creatures to avoid daylight, to make them less vulnerable to preda-tors, so if the flight path between their colonies and their feeding grounds is served by sodium street lights, the bats avoid the light and take the long way home, which may expose them to greater risks from birds of prey.

Perhaps, in the future, town councils will invite C-list celebri-ties to turn *off* their lights for Christmas, to celebrate the festive season by plunging all the streets and squares into planet- (and money-) saving darkness. Then as the lights go out, the assembled members of the public will hold up their mobile phones like candles at a vigil.

*

CCTV has become a way of looking at ourselves, and of seeing the banal present crumbling into pixellated myth and horror. The time-stamped images of the toddler James Bulger being led from the New Strand Shopping Centre, while his mother bought lamb chops from A. R. Tyms butchers, will resonate for a generation, but they might have led us to consider how there was an edge to such surveil-lance, a blackout zone in our midst where cameras were far less frequently stationed. The boys who took James from the brightly strip-lit arcades and bargain shops of the Strand headed out into the gloom of February, taking the child on a long and desperate two-and-a-half-mile march through busy streets, where they were picked up again on cameras, but, in the end, some awful escalation of events on that cold evening finally led them on to the railway, near a disused station, the kind of place well known to truanting children and teenagers as a private space, a space where nobody could see you.

There are still darker places, beyond the city's edgelands. Ten years after the Bulger murder, in the summer of 2003, the country was puzzled and disturbed by the disappearance of a doctor called Richard Stevens, who was last seen arriving for work on a Monday morning at the Royal Manchester Children's Hospital. With his jacket on the back of his office chair, his briefcase on his desk and his Audi ticking in the car park, he walked out of his life and was gone. Apart from the CCTV footage of his arrival captured on an antiquated workplace system, he had simply vanished without trace. An international police search turned up nothing, bar a few false sightings and leads: a tourist picked up on CCTV at John Lennon Airport was mistaken for him; he was spotted on a flight to Florida. In the end, Dr Stevens' body was found — six months later and in the dead of winter — by walkers inside a disused slate mine on Coniston Old Man, a dark place beyond the reach of surveillance and high above the distant incandescence and glare to the south. The coroner ruled that he had taken his own life.

Airports

When an erupting volcano beneath Iceland's Eyjafjallajökull glacier turned the northern skies to ash, and Britain was briefly an island again, newspapers were keen to report the eerie silence around our airports. Radio reporters were dispatched to interview the residents of Hounslow about their new-found peace. Dog-walkers, ramblers and painters were found along the busiest flight paths, and their testimonies were intercut with tales of celebrities riding across Europe by taxi to get to their TV studio on time. But what of the plane-spotters? For them, this must have been a terrible silence.

Plane-spotting, unlike trainspotting, is a quintessentially edge-lands pastime. As boys growing up in the Seventies, we remember the thrill of visiting an airport. But we never flew. Like many British children at the time, the closest we got to foreign travel was watching a smart-suited Alan Whicker plane-hopping his way around the world on TV. But at least at Manchester Ringway Airport you could see the planes, watch them taxi, take off, land, note down their numbers and guess their destinations from the logos on their tails. To watch, close up, a transatlantic jet prepare to fly was a taste of true exotica. No wonder the pier-top viewing deck was full of families at weekends or school holidays. All you needed was a pair of binoculars and a notebook, and the world was yours for an afternoon.

The pier-top viewing deck is long gone – a victim of security concerns – and the airport these days is full of families not watching planes but getting in to them to fly to Ibiza or Benidorm. Have the spotters had their day? Drive around the edge of the airport and you find the answer. Between junction 6 of the M56 and the airport tunnels (where Christiano Ronaldo wrote off his Ferrari) is Manchester Airport's official Aviation Viewing Park. Here, the art of spotting has been tamed, commodified. Three raised viewing mounds afford a 180-degree view across the whole airfield, and provide a vantage point for photographers. There are still families here, but this is hardcore spotting, and many visitors are lone males with hi-tech kit. Binoculars and notebook will no longer do. Now you need a short-wave radio to pick up the squawks between pilots and controllers, a long-lens camera with tripod, plus military-style field glasses to catch the registration numbers. For those who need a break from the coalface, there are three cadavers of planes behind the viewing mounds: an Avro RJX, a BEA Trident, and the oddly unsettling severed front half of a Monarch Airlines DC-10, renovated inside to give it a 'genuine on-board feel'. The real jewel, though, is the 1976 BOAC Concorde. The pinnacle of a Seventies plane-spotter's life was to see this in action, or to glance up and miss it, alerted by its supersonic boom. No schoolboy then would have dreamt this was the end of something, rather than its beginning. We all believed that by the time we were middle-aged (if we lived that long) we would be travelling to New York in the time it took to flick through a newspaper. Now this grounded Mancunian Concorde is a venue, available for private tours, corporate 'gala' dinners and weddings.

*

Aviation Viewing Parks are serious places. The website warns: *Please note there is a strict no ball games, frisbees or kites rule. No dogs with the exception of guide dogs. Please do not feed the birds as they are a hazard to aircraft.* There is not much conversation here, just brief exchanges between spotters comparing notes on aircraft, destinations, numbers. In the Seventies it was a harmless hobby. Now, plane-spotting can bring you to the attention of police, governments and investigative journalists. In 2001 fourteen spotters were arrested and charged with espionage outside a Greek Air Force base. And post 9/11, plane-spotters' records were used to demonstrate the CIA's use of 'extraordinary rendition' of suspected terrorists. It all seems so controlled, so technical, so clinical. Where is the spirit of Seventies 'amateur' plane-spotting now?

Drive further round the airport perimeter until you skirt the southern edge of the Wythenshawe housing estates. Here, in a gap between rows of houses, local kids gather by a tall fence on a grass verge. You only realise why they hang out there when the next arrival from Shanghai, Chicago or Charles de Gaulle comes in to land. This is the unofficial Aviation Viewing Park, outside the perimeter and jurisdiction of the airport, where the jumbo jets make their final descent, missing the fence by what looks like a man's height – undercarriage down, engines screaming – and a pack of kids on bikes howls against the undertow. *Welcome to Manchester, where the local time is 4.30 p.m. The weather is cloudy with light rain.*

*

If you see a crowd gathered near an airport's perimeter fence these days, it's more likely to be protesters than plane-spotters. Airports – or their expansion – have become a front line in an ecological battleground. Millions of people pass though the terminal buildings of our larger airports, but if we think of these places as small cities in themselves, then the distant runway margins, supply hangars and fences are their edgelands, seldom seen except from the windows of a taxiing passenger jet. Anxiously, we might register the state of the runway edge, how grasses are growing through cracks in its surface, and the band of pasture that runs alongside it, but these are places we easily forget, part of the twilight sleep of travel.

That changed in the summer of 2007, when the Camp for Climate Action pitched up at Heathrow, on land earmarked for redevelopment as part of the airport's third runway. Suddenly, this edge found itself at the centre of huge media attention. There is an obvious parallel with what happened over a century ago in this country with reservoir construction – homes and schools would be destroyed, fertile land lost, wildlife displaced, even graveyards would be under threat – except of course the obliteration would take the form of a general levelling and covering in concrete and tarmac, rather than inundation. Instead of a watery depth that contains a drowned village, the new runway and its attendant infrastructure would stand – like Heathrow's other runways – as platform for a stark absence, a big sky over lost orchards and allotments and lanes.

The greater good – clean drinking water and proper sanitation for the urban multitudes – prevailed where our reservoirs were concerned, but the arguments for airport expansion today are less morally urgent and certain, more aggressively mercantile. Apologists for expansion would no doubt claim that these are indivisible terms, and that our ability to compete in a global economy ultimately benefits us all. Against this, the rhetoric of age and tradition is added to the compelling environmental arguments; the village of Sipson, overshadowed by plans for the third runway, dates back to at least 1150 (when it was first recorded as Sibweniston). The global future weighed against the deep rooted past: this is absolutely the fault-line, and it runs through all of our edgelands.

*

The airports fell silent for days. It was April and the high pressure slowing down the dispersal of the volcanic ash from Iceland also meant clear spring skies. For those of us who live on a flight path, the background rumble of climbing airliners was absent, and the dawn chorus seemed louder than usual. April is a busy time for birds, with many migrant species arriving from southern Europe and Africa, and across the wider country the hedges and scrubland and waste ground and flooded gravel workings seemed suddenly louder with the liquid songs and trills of newly arrived warblers. They find their touchdown spaces after long journeys along ancient routes, and set about staking their claims and nest-building in the in-between places where their mosaic of habitat hangs on, either though preservation, neglect or forgetfulness.

That rumble of the jet engine was a huge absence. For the residents of places like Hillingdon or the doomed village of Sipson near Heathrow it must have been a welcome one, the frequent, crushing whine of turbines overhead every couple of minutes altering the rhythm of the day profoundly, affecting thoughts, mood and speech. But for the majority of us, doesn't the low rumble of aircraft adjust our sense of space, making the day feel bigger, higher? The blue of the skies stood unbroken for days, the chalky scribble of jet contrails five miles above completely dissipated. It felt like a blip, or a glimpse into a post-jet age our children's children might come to know, a silence and blueness we once called airspace; how the steady blink of a port-wing light in the evening sky once reminded us of elsewheres and oceans. As Camus wrote of Manhattan in his American journal: 'Sometimes, from beyond the skyscrapers, the cry of a tugboat finds you in your insomnia, and you remember this desert of iron and cement is an island.'

The drifting dust from the Eyjafjallajökull glacier, and the chiff-chaffs and willow warblers, were both telling us something about England that April. Neither respected any of our human borders and boundaries, airspaces or extents of the realm. Next to them, our airports seemed impossibly fixed and leaden, and the only thing certain was that the world would move on from them, as it has done from ports since human time began.

Weather

Just as the world neatly divides into people who have peeled the rubbery rind off a golf ball in order to find out what it's made of, and those who haven't, so there are people who have always wanted to open up and peek inside the white louvre shutters of a Stevenson Screen, and those who haven't.

It looks like an abandoned art installation in the landscape, or a holy site of worship. Electric druids who had recourse to B&Q. Tuned in to and highly sensitive of its surroundings, it feels physically apart from them, although it's easily passed by and overlooked. It's quiet in the low hills to the east of the M6 near Lancaster, apart from the odd car tooling down the back lanes hidden by hedges; the distant, soft, constant roar of the motorway; a dog barking in the boarding kennels you passed on the way up. Before our evening weather bulletins, following on from the news, before the effortless, studied or graceless handovers from news anchor to weather person, before the country is seen as a shiny whole, as if from the height of an observational satellite, before predictions are made with much priestly gesticulation and the sweeping of hands, before all that come places like this: a weather station a hundred or so metres above, and a few miles inland from, Morecambe Bay.

*

Weather stations can – indeed, have to – be found scattered everywhere across the country, although the physical interference created by the human-built environment means their sites tend to favour out-of-the-way edgelands, where they are also less likely to interfere with a view. Not that many people *see* them. From a car, maybe a mast set back from the road, a strange obelisk, and what looks like a beehive on stilts. Then it's gone.

All weather stations are at once different and the same. Different, in elevation and aspect, local topography, the method of information capture – some are live and linked to the Met Office, providing hourly, synoptic readings, others have an archival function – but similar in the deployment of standard operating features and kit you'd expect from a unit that exists solely to provide clean and accurate climate data for analysis. The whole set-up is like a capillary action between the elemental and the empirical, a place where sea mist rolling in off the bay or a blustery shower is being translated into raw information.

In a manual station, it's also a kind of landlocked lighthouse-keeping, a real edgelands job. Somebody has to be here – in this case, every morning at nine o'clock – to make the vital observations. Morning rounds with one gigantic patient.

This one has a shed, which, like all the best sheds, is busy inside with arcane clutter: superannuated meteorological equipment, a grey metal locker full of torches and spare wellies, a computer workstation. The implausible phone does occasionally ring. A few times in the course of a year, somebody will need to know exactly what the weather was doing locally at a given time. Loss adjusters and insurers query the sudden shower that is claimed to have turned a road greasy, or the strong sunlight that dazzled a rear-view mirror and blinded a driver. The weather station itself might be overlooked and unseen, but it is constantly vigilant and recording.

The site is dominated by a 29-metre mast, secured with metal hawsers, a lone starling singing at its tip; an O2 mobile mast – smaller, railed off and crowned in smaller dishes, screens and spiky aerials like a metal fetish statue – squats in its shadow, a shadow that, when the sun is low, you can imagine needling across miles of open country. We begin our rounds.

Climate is recorded slowly, over time, an imperceptible, glacial drip. A weather station, looked at closely from the ground, might also record our capacity for imagining and test our ability to wonder. Memories of long-ago freezing bored field trips are perhaps re-engaged; a horror of clipboards. It just looks like a scattering of vaguely familiar but oddly abstract constructions. The turf-wall rain gauge, a bricked-off, circular indentation a few feet in diameter with some kind of nozzle or aperture at its centre, like a small civic fountain that has dried up and grassed over; anemometers spinning slowly like failed garden appliances; a brick plinth like a deluded, low-level trig point, or a garden centre altar to sun worship.

*

The imperatives of global warming mean that amateur weather enthusiasts – previously bracketed with other British eccentrics like collectors of jam labels or men with narrow-gauge railways in their back gardens – are now feted as eco-heroes. Kids make simple rainfall gauges at primary school and set them up in the back garden. Pensioners hang thermometers outside the kitchen window, and peer out in the morning to read the mercury. But amateur forecasters no longer need rely on barometers like wall clocks, tapping on the glass each time they pass. Now high-street stores sell digital home weather stations, complete with read-outs of temperature, humidity, pressure and a handy icon like the TV weather forecast to tell you whether cloud, rain or sun is on its way. Some even have an audible storm warning, to wake you in the middle of the night so you can watch a storm. Not only do these home weather stations tell you the temperature in your kitchen, they also include at least one external sensor, to be nailed to the wall of your shed, which sends constant readings back to your kitchen to keep you abreast of any changes.

For an amateur weather enthusiast to make the news, though, they need to be a cut above the average record-keeper. In the mid-Noughties a retired paper-maker from Kirkcaldy made the newspapers when the Royal Meteorological Society got interested in his notebooks. Mr David Grisenthwaite had kept a detailed record of when he had cut the grass in his garden for the previous twenty years. The story these records told – that the grass-cutting period had extended by a month in two decades – has become part of the scientific debate on the pace and implications of climate change.

But Mr Grisenthwaite is not alone in his rigorous record-keeping. The science of phenology is enjoying a boom at the moment. Phenology is the study of the seasonal patterns of weather, plant and animal life, which is rooted in long-term and accurate keeping of as many records as possible. In autumn 2000 the UK Phenology Network was set up by the Woodland Trust and the Centre for Ecology and Hydrology to promote this amateur record-keeping to as wide an audience as possible. They now have upwards of 50,000 recruits keeping records: the first flowering of horse chestnut, first flowering of hawthorn, first arrival of swallow, first recorded flight of orange-tip butterfly.

*

Everybody knows the Beaufort Scale, but it's surprising just how much meteorology on the ground relies on scales of observation.

The 'state of ground' patch, a small plot of earth never raked or hoed and tended free of weeds and grasses, like a grave. The tubes and fastenings of ground thermometers only thicken the plot: a Seventies premature-burial kidnapping. The patch is examined every day, like the inspection of a tiny sports pitch or course to see if play or a meet is possible, and like everything observed here it is graded according to preordained categorisations, coded on a scale that runs from 'frozen' or 'drenched' through 'moist' to 'dry'. Visibility is measured by landmarks: towers or buildings at known distances are quickly clocked and recorded. It's almost the opposite of the proverbial and pastoral folkloric forecast: 'Red sky at night, shepherd's delight.' You forecast in poetry, but you collect data in prose.

But some of the measuring equipment installed in weather stations is ingenious and beautiful. The tipping-bucket rain-gauge, hidden just below ground, collects rainwater on small measuring scales that tip when full and can be linked to sensors, making it fully automatic: a device so mechanically simple and resourceful it seems to connect the world of Al-Jazari and the Arabic Middle Ages with the world of the semiconductor. The Campbell-Stokes sunshine recorder is even more elegant: a glass crystal ball, mounted facing south, that tracks the movement and power of the sun across the sky by burning a moving hole across a sheet of time-graded card. Throughout the year, three seasonal cards need to be used, depending on the angle of the sun, and weather-station recorders learn the rhythms of these cards, looking forward to when the winter card will be replaced by the equinoctial card as much as the rest of us might welcome the clocks going forward. On sunny days there is a fresh, scorched smell hanging in the air like incense when the sunshine recorder is approached.

*

And then there is the Stevenson Screen. A white (to reflect solar radiation) wooden box, its door faces north and its walls are double-louvred (to permit a stable airflow). It was designed by Thomas Stevenson to create a stable environment in which to site tempera-ture and barometric pressure-measuring equipment, though Stevenson was better known in his day as a lighthouse designer, as were his brothers and his father Robert Stevenson, who was also a builder of roads; but one of his sons, Robert Louis Stevenson, broke with this dynastic, paternal vocation of scientific engineering and lighthouse-building. It caused a great deal of bitterness within the family.

And yet. The Stevenson who wrote *The Strange Case of Dr Jekyll and Mr Hyde* and *Treasure Island* was originally trained as an engi-neer. His earliest published work was a paper — 'On the Thermal Influence of Forests' — presented to the Royal Society of Edinburgh in 1873. The engineering achievements of his father and uncles and grandfather underwrote the writing life Stevenson undertook, and there's plenty of evidence to suggest he was keenly aware of this, and of the discrepancy between those towering achievements and his own smaller literary accom-plishments. Not that the world saw it that way: in 1886 Stevenson wrote an angry letter to Scribner's complaining at the lack of public recognition his father had received, comparing his own fame and success:

. . . I might write books till 1900 and not serve humanity so well; and it moves me to a certain impatience, to see the little, frothy bubble that attends the author his son, and compare it with the obscurity in which that better man finds his reward.

Around the same time, Stevenson wrote the poem 'Skerryvore: the Parallel'. 'Skerryvore' was the name of the house in Bournemouth that Thomas Stevenson bought for his son's wife; Skerryvore itself was the name of a rocky reef to the west of Mull that had claimed many ships, until a lighthouse was erected there by Alan Stevenson, the novelist's uncle.

> Here all is sunny, and when the truant gull
> Skims the green level of the lawn, his wing
> Dispetals roses; here the house is framed
> Of kneaded brick and the plumed mountain pine,
> Such clay as artists fashion and such wood
> As the tree-climbing urchin breaks. But there
> Eternal granite hewn from the living isle
> And dowelled with brute iron, rears a tower
> That from its wet foundation to its crown
> Of glittering glass, stands, in the sweep of winds,
> Immovable, immortal, eminent.

Later, in the Samoan Isles, Stevenson, while working on his *Records of a Family of Engineers*, wrote home asking for his father's engineering pocket book: 'I cannot do without it.' In some complex way, Stevenson always fretted over the usefulness or true value of art, art compared to the practical, life-and-death construction work of the engineer. Strange now that even the lighthouses of our inshore waters are all automated and unmanned, though his father's simple and elegant screen for meteorological instruments is still an absolutely standard piece of kit.

What's worth more in the end: art or practical utility? As Matthew Arnold put it: 'Doors that open, windows that shut, locks that turn, razors that shave, coats that wear, watches that go, and a thousand more such good things, are the invention of the Philistines.'

*

Edgelands do weather very well. The aesthetics of weather are enhanced by the forms and colours of the place. Rain at night is often beautiful, but look at slant rain at night, falling on a fenced-off yard full of identically liveried vans or brand-new cars, lit by powerful security lights; the multiple tones and rhythms of torrential rain on metal roofs and doors. Then there are the squalls of rain that blow across a motorway to settle over pools of unnamed standing water, rattling through the scrappy copses beside the water. As Paul Muldoon says in his early poem 'Wind and Tree', 'most of the wind / Happens where there are trees'.

But it's not just rain. Have you seen the sudden, filmic light effects of low winter sun across a ruined factory, the hard-cut shadows and blinding reflections off broken glass? Late-afternoon sun on a clear day throwing giant shadows like ink fields on the scrubland behind power station cooling towers? Or milk morning sun brushing the tops of willowherb, nettle, thistle, in the unkempt field behind the car-crushers? Perhaps it is because we are so used to seeing the edgelands used as a movie set that this angled sunlight seems so dramatic, so designed.

And is it the brokenness of the edgelands that renders them so susceptible to weather, so apparently responsive to it? Many people with broken bones will claim, years after the break has healed, that they can still tell when the weather is about to turn by an ache at the point of the fracture. Muldoon's poem 'Wind and Tree' goes on to describe two trees, entangled by the wind:

257

Their branches that are grinding
Madly together and together,

It is no real fire.
They are breaking each other.

Often I think I should be like
The single tree, going nowhere,

Since my own arm could not and would not
Break the other. Yet by my broken bones

I tell new weather.

*

While not as birdy as some edgelands places (cf. sewage farms),
weather stations nevertheless seem to be good places to watch avian
comings and goings. Maybe it's the general observational frame of
mind we're in, or the shed – if there is one – that easily doubles as
a hide, or simply all of those posts and masts and plinths available
for perching, that makes a place like this feel a bit like an unofficial bird reserve. It's too early in the year here for the curlews and
oystercatchers and lapwings, which are still feeding out in the estu-
aries of the bay, but atop the mast, a starling continues to work its
way through a low-key, late-winter version of its collaged song, a
cut-and-paste job made out of curlew calls, assorted rattles and
hisses and metallic clicks.

Starlings are keen mimics, the mynah birds of the north (to which
they are related). They're the samplers among our avifauna, able to
incorporate all manner of human, animal and mechanical sounds

into their repertoire, and urban starlings are well-known copyists of telephones and doorbells, even dial-up modems. The song-learning process in birds is well studied, but still somewhat mysterious: researchers in this field believe that understanding the neural mechanisms that underlie imitative song-learning is the Holy Grail. But imagine a starling that enriches its individual repertoire by imitating some distinct and regular mechanical noise. This ability might crystallise into the vocal performance of a mature adult, and so might also be copied both by direct offspring and other impressionable, immature birds looking to extend their own vocal abilities. Starlings have been observed at abandoned human settlements recreating the noises of former human or mechanical activity: a squeaky water pump, even though the pump is long seized up, or the rasp of a bandsaw, even though the woodshed is long deserted. Could it be that the starlings that gather here sing a song made from bits of the area's former soundscape? These low hills were once the site of much industrial activity, dating back to Roman times, and the landscape hereabouts is littered with the sites of limekilns and forges. Dirty, unpleasant work. The area has always been a kind of edgelands, but could it be possible that starlings still carry within their complicated songs some of the sound elements of that former industrial world? Thought of this way, the birds themselves are a kind of information storage system, a winged databank.

★

The spring of 2010, and the first signs that iPhone birdsong apps are being abused, as people begin to play the pre-recorded warblings and alarm calls of various confused species back into the trees and bushes. We see the first occurrences of a new kind of edgelands flash mob: at first light, hundreds gather in the silent places outside of towns and cities, lit by the firefly glow of their phone screens, and at the preordained exact moment play the songs of their chosen birds, a digital dawn chorus made possible by lightweight flash-memory technology.

*

Later in the day, starlings begin to assemble in long minatory Hitchcockian strings along the mast's cables. As evening approaches, they take to the air as one and gather into the swarming shapes familiar from our city centres and beer commercials, heading north towards the huge winter flock that forms near the Lune. Maybe because they form such huge murmurations, starlings are more broadly local, learning each other's calls and exchanging information in the vast shoalings we see at dusk. According to meteorologists, there are three types of twilight: civil twilight, once the sun has sunk six degrees below the horizon; nautical twilight, when the sun is twelve degrees deep and the horizon is difficult to discern; and astronomical twilight, once the sky has turned completely dark. But there is also starling twilight, that uncanny borderline moment when the birds' collective mind decides it is time to fall into its night-time roost, and the great display comes to its sudden and mysterious end.

Piers

So where do the edgelands end? How far can the idea take us? As an island people, we have our own ideas of edges, and between the specifically English *urban* of the seaside town, and the wilds of the ocean beyond it, we have developed our own very particular coastal edgelands.

*

Piers, all our lives. A region's tapering extremity, pieces of England stepping in to the snotgrey Irish Sea, making short-lived, reckless attempts at *entente* in the Channel, enduring the freezing manacles of the North Sea. Like the halls of mirrors some of them once hosted, piers are full of space and many-edged: it's easy to feel the footfall of a century of day-trippers and holidaymakers, funnelled along their boardwalks, the shortfall between a postcard's saturated brilliance and the blistered craquelure and grey sea, the swing and band tunes and beat music submerged under the poptones of the present. Gusts carry the smells of caramelised sugars and oils at smoking point and fried onions, mixed with the scent of the sea itself, and we know we've been here before, in another life.

*

The underside of piers is another world. As a child, these dark, dripping strips of sand and sea are irresistible. However much gentrification or modernisation a sun-side pier has undergone, its belly always looks ancient, decayed, like a beached shipwreck. Even in the height of summer (well, as high as an English summer gets) it is cold enough to cause a shiver here, as you cross from the open beach. The sand is compacted and cold underfoot. The vast weed- and limpet-covered legs are rooted deep, and the farthest of them stand half in water. Steady lines of drips from the last high tide make this feel like a caving trip, and as you walk to where the waves lap, you can just see the fishermen's lines, like a soon-to-fail attempt to tether the tide to the pier.

Did you talk to the fishermen when you walked up there? They don't like to say much. As the Australian poet Les Murray says in his poem 'The Fishermen at South Head', 'It is serious to be with humans':

> Through their horizontal poles they divine the creatures of
>   ocean:
> a touch, a dip, and a busy winding death gets started;
> hands will turn for minutes, rapidly,
> before, still opening its pitiful doors, the victim
> dawns above the rim, and is hoisted in a flash above
>   the suburbs
> – or before the rod flips, to stand
> trailing sworn-at gossamer.

*

As the sea temperatures struggle towards tolerable levels, we enter the tombstoning season again. Tombstoning is simply jumping from height into the sea, either from cliffs, breakwaters, harbour walls, or piers. Kids have always jumped into the waves, but since it gained a name, and with a global audience watching on YouTube, this seasonal activity also has the contours of a craze. It's a nascent sport, in the process of trying to promote wetsuits, tide knowledge and greater awareness; though it is also still a whim, a dare, a drunken spur-of-the-moment deal. Every summer, the newspapers carry stories of fatalities or serious injuries from all around our coastline.

At the very edge of the country, here is one way of achieving peer-group status, notoriety and a pure adrenaline rush. Piers are among the most inviting of springboards for a jump, but also the most dangerous, as tides can pull the jumper out to open sea quickly, or smash them against the iron legs and supports. It's common for tombstoners to scream as they fall, as if their captive souls have been reintroduced to the wild, albeit only for a second or two, before they hit the water. Jumpers are advised to tuck their arms in, especially if they attempt a plummet while holding their nose: the force of impact can cause them to punch themselves in the face, very hard.

*

We visit the abandoned West Pier at Brighton, just months before it suffers a fatal collapse and a series of fires and is closed. We're obliged to wear hard hats and life jackets as we're led on to the promenade, closed to the general public since 1975. Rain taps our heads. We cross a series of walkways above the jungle of girders and rotten boards, the sea calm and well behaved, though it's unnerving to look down through the slats. The pavilions are gloomy inside, and even though most of the glazing has gone, they are filled with an ammoniacal stink so bad that scarves and lapels are pulled up as masks. The interiors are covered in bird guano, the floor space littered with dead pigeons and starlings that have built up and formed a kind of feathery jam.

In the Pavilion Theatre, furthest from shore, we find the shell of Laughterland, with its admission prices still painted on the wall in old money, and disconcerting images of clowns. This space would have once been filled with bandits and penny falls and teddy grabbers, and we imagine the coins that have passed through here on their long orbits in the world. Places like this would have been their furthest journeys from the mint that struck them, where they still (just) carried spending power and the sympathetic magic of the quick thrill, the little squirts of hope, pleasure and disappointment.

Later, we wait for the starlings to come, returning to this roost from points all along the coast. We watch the swarm cloud build, flexing and trawling through the dusk until at no particular moment it descends on the pavilion, entering through its many missing panes and voids. If we were back inside Laughterland at this moment, as insubstantial as one of the arcade's many ghosts, this incoming flow of birds would surely be spectacular and torrential, black grain from a hopper. The bird has an etymological link with money: the synecdochic 'sterling' has uncertain origins, but one theory is that early British silver coinage was hallmarked with starlings, which were then called 'stearlings'. By the time we looked back at the photographs we'd taken that day, months later, the West Pier had burned. We notice for the first time that the interior of Laughterland was painted a very watery blue, the colour, in fact, of a starling's egg.

Acknowledgements

We were both gathering materials for this book long before we knew there was a book to write, and so we acknowledge the company and conversation of umpteen chance encounters and acquaintances – business travellers and staff in hotels and motorway services, pigeon fanciers, allotment holders, anglers, boy racers, landscape gardeners – who all, in their various ways, nudged us in the direction of the edgelands, and *Edgelands*. And we should mention how, before them, lies the landscape of childhood, and its cast of thousands. But once we had a book in mind, specific help was called for, and we wish to express our gratitude to the following people: Martin Bence, Edward Chell, Kate Clanchy, Mark Cocker, Tim Dee, Tim Edensor, David Gilroy, Niall Griffiths, Emma Harding, Debra Hurst, Henry Iddon, Karen Lockney, Neil McCarthy, Clive McWilliam, Mike Marley, Professor Lenny Moss, Saleel Nurbhai, Jacob Polley, Richard Purslow, the staff of Ratcliffe-on-Soar power station, Stephen Regan, Ruth Roberts, Carole Romaya, Leila Romaya, Marion Shoard, Mark Simmons and Julian Turner.

Thanks also to our agents, David Godwin and Peter Straus, who have provided invaluable counsel, and to the team at Jonathan Cape who have assisted and supported us every step of the way, especially Tom Avery, Clara Womersley, and above all our editor Robin Robertson.

'Letter to Lord Byron' and 'New Year Letter' from *Collected Poems* by W. H. Auden. Copyright © 1936, 2001, The Estate of W. H. Auden. Extract from 'Black Country' exhibition catalogue reproduced by kind permission of Richard Billingham. 'The Map' from *The Complete Poems 1927-79* by Elizabeth Bishop. Copyright © 1979, 1983 by Alice Helen Methfessel. Reprinted by permission of Farrar, Straus and Giroux, LLC. Quotations from www.blessitt.com reproduced by kind permission of Arthur Blessitt. Extract from 'The narrow world of Norman Cornish' by Sid Chaplin, published in the *Guardian* newspaper on 24 May 1960. Copyright © *Guardian* News and Media Ltd. 'The Clay-Tip Worker' by Jack Clemo, taken from *Jack Clemo, Selected Poems* published by Bloodaxe Books. Courtesy of the Bill Douglas Centre for the History of Cinema and Popular Culture, University of Exeter. Extract from *Industrial Ruins: Space, Aesthetics and Materiality*